D0500079

THE VIKINGS
IN
BRITAIN

For Pat

THE VIKINGS
IN
BRITAIN

H. R. LOYN

Professor of Medieval History
University College, Cardiff

St. Martin's Press
New York

Acknowledgements

The object of this book is to provide an account of the Viking Invasions of Britain in relatively short space which puts the movement into a truly British perspective. Inevitably this has meant I have had to rely on the good services of many scholars expert in a variety of disciplines. I pay special acknowledgement to my friends in the Viking Society and the English Place-Name Society who have helped make this book possible by their own published work and encouragement, to Professor Michael Dolley for his ever-ready help on numismatic problems, especially in relation to the illustrations on plate 7, to Professor David Wilson and Mrs Lesley Webster for help with the archaeological illustrations, and to Dr Justin Schove for help with all matters relating to climatic problems. We are grateful to the British Museum, to the Director of the Royal Coin Cabinet and Museum for Monetary History at Stockholm, to Mr A. L. Binns, to Mrs Alan Sorrell and the Department of the Environment, the Nationalmuseet, Copenhagen, and the Universitets Oldsaksamling, Oslo, for permission to use illustrative material. My greatest debt is to my wife to whom the book is formally dedicated both for creating conditions in which writing is possible and for constructing the index.

H. R. Loyn

Cardiff, March 1977

Library of Congress Catalog Card Number: 77–73918
ISBN: 0–312–84671–1
First published in the United States of America in 1977

Contents

Illustrations

1.

The Scandinavian World and Europe in the Early Viking Age

The making of modern Europe was a slow and laborious business which the historian simplifies at peril. Modern conceptions of national growth and of national types are too easily applied to situations in the past where they are distorting, anachronistic and positively misleading. To be obsessed with the image of peaceful and peace-loving Scandinavian farmers, taken from the history of Scandinavia over the last two centuries, can lead to falsification as great as that provoked by the nursery and early schoolboy image of ruthless Viking axemen, horn-helmeted and heathen, breakers of skulls and despoilers of churches. Reality was much more complex. Not all farmers love peace. A ravager in May can turn a skilful hand to corn-harvest in August. One of the main objects of this book is to point to the highly complex human situation of raid and settlement, of piracy and cultivation that we mask under the conveniently smooth description of the Viking Age.

This Viking Age with its rough chronological extent from 800 to 1100 had a tremendous effect on the making of modern Europe. The process of recovery from the economic dislocation and political disaster which attended the fall of the Roman Empire in the West was not far advanced when the fresh wave of barbarian invasion struck. The historian, and especially the social and economic historian with his knowledge of happenings still to come, can see that this recovery was more than recovery, that Europe was proliferating in new growth, that the Carolingian world was different from and in many ways superior to the late Classical world it aped and thought to be reconstituting. But when Charles the Great was crowned emperor in the basilica of St Peter's at Rome by Pope Leo III on Christmas Day, 800, to many contemporaries it must have seemed a symbol of recovery, a sign that the barbarian was tamed, that Rome

7

had survived and triumphed in the West at Rome as in the East at Constantinople. Charles, king of the Franks and of the Lombards, greatest of the Germanic warchiefs had re-established the *imperium christianum* of Constantine. The warriors of the Christian king of the Franks, now hailed as emperor, protected the Danube frontier. The Rhine was no longer a frontier. Frankish soldiers, Christian missionaries (especially Anglo-Saxons) and papal emissaries brought faith and sometimes peace to the continental German lands as far as the Elbe and the Harz mountains in the east, and to the borders of Denmark in the north. An amalgam of German and Roman had been triumphantly achieved in the name of Christ. North Africa, Egypt, and the greater part of Spain, and Jerusalem and Syria were, it is true, in Mohammedan hands, but there were signs that the centre of power in the Moslem world was moving east. It was from Baghdad and not from Damascus that the Caliph Haroun-al-Raschid conducted his correspondence and despatched his embassies to the Frankish Charles. At Constantinople, Irene, the empress of the second Rome, watched uneasily the progress of the Franks in the West. The Eastern Empire, as it now may be called, possessed political control of Asia Minor, and by constant labour retained its foothold in the south of Italy, Sicily, and the islands of the Eastern Mediterranean. Its strength, and increasingly its reason of being, lay in Constantinople, Miklegarth, the great city, as the Vikings were to come to term it, the pivot of world trade between west and east. Now in the face of the two world blocks that had emerged from the ruins of Rome, Byzantium and the Moslem Empire, the West also had precariously achieved its unity, a new unity it might be said, with a literal reorientation. The continental Germans, Saxons, Thuringians, Bavarians, Suabians, and Franconians had been brought within the pale of Romanic, Christian civilization. A third world force had been created.[1] Frankish counts and Christian bishops, *comites episcopique*, were brought to the fringe of territories inhabited by hostile Slavs and powerful Northerners. Byzantium would penetrate culturally much though not all of the Slav territory. Western concerns now lay increasingly with the West Slavs, Wends, Poles, Czechs, Slovaks, and – the central point in our story – with the Scandinavians.

Such broad and sweeping generalisations have their moments of truth and also their dangers. From the ethnic point of view it is only too easy to see the period 400–800 as the time when the German peoples, including the Anglo-Saxons, were converted to a Roman-based civilised way of life with the Christian church, the heir of Rome, acting as the principal agent. Our Viking Age then is the next stage forward. By 1100 the Christian religion was accepted in

Greenland, in Iceland, and throughout the Scandinavian world. Christian dynasties that looked to Rome were dominant among the Poles, the Czechs, and even the non-Slavonic Hungarians. The centralised and centralising papacy of Hildebrand, Pope Gregory VII, 1073–85, influenced a wider territory than that embraced in the western part of the territorial state of Rome. Who were these Northerners, the Scandinavians, so painfully brought into the orbit of Christendom? What standard of civilisation had they reached at the time of the coronation of Charles the Great? Why were they about to constitute at that stage in European development a new and fearful threat to the Western world? These are the questions which have provoked so much recent thought and writing on the Northern world.

Scandinavia towards the end of the 8th century

There is very little historical evidence in the strict sense of the term which we can use to describe affairs in Scandinavia at this time. References from written Western sources deal mostly with raids and were naturally written from the point of view of the victims. A coherent narrative account can scarcely be reconstructed from such references. Scandinavia itself, apart from the use of runic letters in carved memorial stones and on wood, was illiterate, a brutal fact forgotten at peril by one wishing to make a just evaluation of the state of development of the communities dwelling therein. Later written evidence, in prose and poetry, dealing with the period in the Old Norse tongue, is often highly coloured, written with an eye to literary effect rather than historical accuracy, and yet valuable in that it contains some firm outlines of tradition among peoples accustomed to oral transmission of evidence. Our picture depends mostly, however, on the evidence of what the historian used to call in his arrogance the ancillary sciences, ancillary, that is to say, to the pure historical record of the written word: archaeology, linguistics, and the allied disciplines of place-name study. For the particular set of problems connected with Scandinavia proper at this time other scientists, too, have their contributions to make, notably the student of climatic changes.

From the patient work of many scholars operating in their various disciplines it is possible to say something of the peoples of Scandinavia in the 8th century and of their organisation. The archaeologist, in particular, has made tremendous contributions, and without the investigations of a succession of able men from Steenstrup and Bugge to Brøndsted, Arbman, and their successors, our knowledge would be very thin.

9

It is clear that we have some justification in treating Scandinavia as a whole in spite of the vast extent of territory concerned, and in spite too of the great diversity in geographical structure and economic development. Whatever their ultimate origins and whatever the degree of mixture of bloods, the dominant group was Germanic in race and in language. They were not all the blond, blue-eyed giants of popular myth, but they contained within their number a high proportion of such tall fair people. Our knowledge of the time taken by human groups to adapt themselves to climatic and ecological conditions is still in its infancy, but it does seem likely that the Scandinavians had reached a stage in their evolution by the 8th century A.D. when one would expect such a type to begin to predominate. Many prehistorians date the presence of recognisable ancestors of the historic Germanic peoples of Scandinavia to the middle of the first millennium B.C., and have associated their presence with a possible climatic change which brought Scandinavia from a period of dry sunny summers and long mild winters to the sub-Atlantic conditions of cool damp summers and harsh winters which have prevailed with important variations (which included a prolonged period of improved weather conditions which reached an optimum in the eleventh and twelfth centuries A.D.) to this day. New techniques applied to the sometimes intangible and sometimes diffuse evidence bring the dating of this major climatic change into some doubt, but it is salutary to seize on the main firm conclusion: the pine forests now taken as a fundamental element in Scandinavian ecology came at some point of time, most probably towards the end of the second millennium and within the first half of the first millennium B.C., to predominate over the mixed deciduous forests, including oak and beech, of the more congenial earlier Bronze Age. Worsening climatic conditions within the sub-Atlantic type may have prompted a degree of migration south from Scandinavia and the Baltic area of the ancestors of some of our well-known tribes of Germanic history: legend would place a movement of some at least of the elements of the later federations known as Goths and Burgundians among their number at a date about 200 B.C. when the climate was entering a fairly warm phase. It is certain that at the very end of the 2nd century B.C., in 101 B.C., the Germanic tribes known as the Cimbri and the Teutons raided through central Europe from their Scandinavian homelands, only to be decisively defeated by the Romans. The influence of the Roman Empire proved great in commercial and cultural fields, though no direct attempt at conquest was made. As part of the Germanic folk-wandering of the 5th century A.D. a migration occurred when large numbers, particularly from modern Denmark, but also containing some groups from Sweden, moved west into Frisia and England. Bede, a careful collector of information about the antecedents of the English race, wrote in the early 8th century that the Angles (who came from Angeln in Schleswig) had come in such numbers that their province, lying between the land of the Old Saxons and the land of the Jutes, remained deserted to his very own day. Evidence from pagan cemeteries points to depopulation attendant upon migration. Undoubtedly the folk movements of the 5th century left Scandinavia underpopulated with more land than the survivors could cope with. The 6th and 7th centuries, and to a considerable extent the 8th also, represent a quiet period in Scandinavian political history, probably associated with the beginnings of a period of climatic amelioration. Rich grave finds from the Vendel period, notably in Sweden at Old Uppsala and at Helgö in Lake Mälar indicate some trading contacts south with the Merovingian and the Mediterranean world; in these areas there is proof of intense if not widespread prosperity among political leaders and some merchants. There are isolated reports of raids, one made by the warrior king Hygelac into Frisia, *c.* 520, having a special interest for English students, as Hygelac (Chlochilaicus in Gregory of Tours) is the king of the Geats, uncle and patron of the epic hero Beowulf. It is commonly and probably correctly supposed that the literary silence of these centuries is a fair reflection of events dominated by the problems of internal colonisation, with no time or energy for external aggression. Again we know only too little of the time taken by human groups to exploit new lands: analogies with later colonisation movements in Canada or Siberia can be helpful but only if we take into account the massive technical strides taken by mankind between the 6th and the eighteenth centuries A.D. Pasturage for the beasts, water free of ice for communications and for fishing, land for the plough, were the essentials probably in that order; protection against beast and man – the justification for political organisation – became a further pressing need as the groups settled and prospered.

Awareness of a working homogeneity persisted among these groups. This was strengthened by a common religion, the product, no doubt, of such of the intellectual effort as could be spared from the fight against nature. Reconstruction of the detail of their religious practices is matter for the anthropologist as well as for the archaeologist. Evidence and influence from burial customs and place-names and from the language itself give the basis of reasonable conclusions. The Scandinavians were a branch of the Germanic peoples and many of their beliefs were rooted in a common Germanic past:

burial ceremonies, fertility rites, the very names of the gods, the principal among which still survive throughout the Germanic world in the familiar names of the days of the week – Tiw, Woden (Odin), Thor and Frigg who gave their names to Tuesday, Wednesday, Thursday and Friday. It is evident, however, that a special twist was given both to their belief and to their ceremonies by the peculiar climatic and economic situation they found themselves enjoying in the Northern world. In matters of belief the hard necessity of reliance on self and companions in the often bitter struggle against Northern nature led to a curious attitude of equality towards the gods. The Viking did not creep to the altar. The gods themselves were subject to testing, and open to rejection when a stronger than they appeared. In ceremony, simplification, or perhaps more strictly, failure to elaborate, seems to have been the dominant theme. There are accounts of occasional formal sacrificial ceremonies. Viking ship-burial represents one of the most elaborate forms known to mankind for the disposal of the body of the dead. Everyday routine and seasonal change were accompanied by religious ceremonial. But a specialist priesthood did not develop. The king possessed a sacral quality, and each head of household possessed sacrificial rights; but there is little trace of a class of men set apart from other men by their professional career for worship of the gods. In the hard climate of the North, such luxuries could not be afforded: men were needed at battle, plough and bed.

The Scandinavians were polytheistic. A multiplicity of gods governed the cycle of the years. Some strong elements of nature worship persisted and were further to persist until and beyond the end of heathendom. Fountains, streams and graves were regarded as specially sacred. Cults were built around veneration for the oak or the ash. The heavens in their mysteries, sun, moon, thunder and lightning, attracted the worshipper. In more sophisticated form regeneration themes can faintly be traced in the attitudes to the rising sun on the cycle of human growth from conception to death and decay. By the opening of the Viking Age three cults were clearly coming to predominate within the Northern pantheon: the worship of Woden (Odin), Thor and Frey. Under stress of the Viking Age and ceaseless activity Thor came to predominate, notably in Iceland, though Odin continued to draw much support, notably from the articulate poets and nobles who cared for wisdom, even for the wisdom of the serpent, more than for strength. In essence Thor was a sky-god, Jove the Thunderer. His symbols were the hammer, the axe, and probably the swastika. Physical strength was his prime attribute. He regulated the weather. Seafarers turned to him in their peril. Woden (Odin in the North) developed into a much more sophisticated being, though originally he was in all probability no more than the god of War, or Mars, giver of victory in battle. In the North be became the god of cunning in the full sense of the word, knowledge as well as craft. He was the god who would beguile the wayfarer, the one-eyed to be encountered at cross-roads, the wily protector. Frey was the fertility god, hermaphroditic in most elaborate form, protector of crops, of sex and the harvest. There is some evidence that his cult was more fully developed in Sweden than any of the other Scandinavian communities.

Other gods and supernatural beings also abounded and are among the best known figures of Scandinavian thought to the modern world. Balder, the beautiful and Loki, the evil genius of the gods, are known to us as well as, if not better than, the figures of Greek mythology. But they are the product of the high imagination of a sophisticated literary civilisation of the twelfth and thirteenth centuries. They represent the triumph of antiquarian reconstruction. As such, our Tales from Asgarth tell us much of the fine achievements of Icelandic civilisation; they only reflect dimly, and sometimes distort grossly, the gods of the Viking Age.

The same must be said of the fundamental tenets of belief of the Scandinavian. In finished literary form, as seen through the writings of Snorri Sturluson, the Scandinavians had a most elaborate mythology. Man's struggle in this world was an incident, an episode, on his way to the next. Essentially it was a testing-time. If the test were successfully taken, the warrior would, after death in battle, weapon in hand, enter Valhalla where a place would be prepared for him. The choosers of the slain would proffer him wine. He would live the life of a chosen companion until the gods would lead him out on the last fight against the snake that encompassed the earth, against the powers of evil. The fight would end in disaster. The Twilight of the Gods would end in deep night. Things won – or lost – were done; all joy lay in the doing. Such myth was the product of long centuries, much influenced by parallel Christian beliefs. Echoes of it can, however, be traced back to the earliest poetry. The boldness and in a sense the completeness of the fully formulated pattern should not blind us to the essential inadequacy and immaturity of the religion for a settled civilised people. Perpetuation of the life of the military camp is a poor ideal to set against the subtler spiritual force of Christianity.

Nevertheless, similarity of belief, even if sometimes tenuously held, served as a unifying force among the Scandinavians. More important perhaps is a cognate similarity in language and institutions.

To talk of language and language change at this precise stage in Scandinavian history is to risk the chance of indulging in airy hypothesis. The inhabitants of Scandinavia were essentially illiterate, and without evidence in writing, knowledge of the spoken tongue is apt to be patchy, surviving merely in fossilised form in place-names and proper names, often preserved by men of alien speech. The illiteracy was not, of course, total and some valuable material does survive from memorial stones, notably those written in the runic alphabet known as *futhark*.[2] It is likely that this alphabet was created about the end of the 2nd or beginning of the 3rd century A.D., and that it represents in fact, derived as it is from Greek, Roman, or possibly North Italian alphabets, a conspicuous civilising move of the type that brought the Gothic Bible into being from the Romanic world to the barbarians without the Empire. Most of these stories and inscriptions survive from the island of Gotland or from the Swedish milieu of Old Uppsala and the Vendel graves. We know that the language spoken was Germanic. Language experts tell us that it differentiated itself from the parent tongue probably before the age of the folk-migration (4th and 5th centuries A.D.), indeed, probably in the period running from the 1st century B.C. to the 1st century A.D. Differences from continental German and notably from West German (with which it retained closest affinities) developed slowly during the Primitive Norse period, *c.* 100 A.D.–700 A.D., but accelerated during the Viking period itself when unaccented vowels tended to disappear and the characteristic mutations occurred.[3] Within the Northern German orbit language variations were very slight, no more than those that exist in modern English dialects. Right through the Viking Age and indeed throughout the Middle Ages, there was no difficulty of communication among the Scandinavians. What changes occurred were precise but not enough to prevent intelligibility. Some regional peculiarity of vocabulary grew and extended. The changes were exact enough for linguistic scholars to separate off Old West Scandinavian and Old East Scandinavian, the past tongues of modern Norwegian and Icelandic on the one hand and of modern Swedish and Danish on the other, certainly from about 1000 A.D., and possibly earlier if the evidence of British place-names can be taken fully into account. But they are slight within the structure of the language as a whole. For all practical purposes only one tongue was spoken in the North at the time of the opening of the Viking Age.

Institutional life is in some respects even more elusive than language change, but here again we can point to some certainties. The Scandinavians knew kingship, not extensive territorial kingship, but the recognised existence of certain kindreds which because of their pre-eminence in war were known as royal. These kindreds enjoyed special legal privileges, and special rights and duties, in large part religious as well as military, were also associated with them. In southern Norway one dynasty, the Ynglinga, had risen to special prominence and dominated the lands around the Oslo fjord. A cognate dynasty had reached the height of political achievement in the prehistoric period in Sweden, and the great grave mounts of Old Uppsala and the Vendel period still testify to its magnificence. We also know of many other dynasties, among the Geats in what is now southern Sweden but was then an integral part of the Danish world, among the Danes themselves at Leire in Zealand, and (with its great days still far in the future) at Jelling in Jutland, around Bergen in the western fjords of Norway, and far to the north among the men of Trondheim. The title of king was much less exclusive than among some of the German peoples of the Western folk-wandering. It was used freely by many male adults of a royal kin. Institutions associated with kingship were weak. The kings lacked the apparatus of dependent local government, and of the tenacious and sometimes blind support of a literate clerisy, without which permanent active life was difficult in these centuries. They were essentially warlords whose wealth and power were sometimes glorious, but often brief and precarious.

There also existed a class of earls or jarls sometimes difficult to distinguish from the king but clearly lacking both the pagan sanctions and the special dignity which went with the royal kindreds. These seem to have been prominent in the Norwegian lands, notably in the fjords of the south-west and west where the sheer isolation of geography may well have led to the emergence of a number of powerful families, not one able to sustain supremacy but all gaining enough from their lordship over several small fjord settlements to raise their families above the commonalty. They also had come by the opening of the Viking Age to enjoy special legal privileges in return presumably for the protection they were able to offer the folk.

The basic unit in society, however, was no king or earl but a *bondir*, a free farmer, roughly equivalent to the Anglo-Saxon ceorl. It is well from the outset to disabuse ourselves of misleading democratic notions. The *bondir* was no little man in our sense of the word. He was at his most typical the head of a household, a man of some property in land and especially in stock. He was a slave-owner. His symbols of rank were his axe and his spear. The mark of the freeman was the right to bear arms. He was oath-worthy and law-worthy with a right to assist at the making of judgements at the local court. Sturdy, and at times savage, independence was a characteristic of this breed, but we must remember how his very litigious and squabblesome nature found its outlet in what was essentially communal institutional life, in the folk-court, the local *thing*, held at some traditional spot in forest, heath or grave, marked by some memorial of stone or wood, hallowed by long custom already by the end of the 8th century.

There was, therefore, a certain unity in social structure characteristic of the whole of the Scandinavian lands at the beginning of the Viking Age. Some of the features were, it is true, common to all the Germanic world, but the economic backwardness and the localism bred of such poverty exaggerated Scandinavian peculiarities: the petty king and earl, the *bondir* and the unfree thrall were the typical units in this Northern society. Only in some favoured areas were these signs of a stirring towards greater things, towards a kingship that would extend over a wider area. The Viking Age can never be seen in proper perspective unless it is realised that the terrifying raids overseas were co-terminous with the first stirrings towards a national unity within Scandinavia itself. We have to this point stressed Scandinavian uniformity. Differences also existed, differences natural to communities which dwelt in habitats as varied as the rugged fjords of the Sogn and Hardanger, the fertile lowlands of Leire or Ribe, or the savage lands of Halgaland, further north than other men dwelt. By 1100 these differences had been given political shape and permanent form by the creation of the three kingdoms of Norway, Sweden and Denmark. In 800 the shape could be discerned, but the permanence was far from certain.

Three dynasties in fact, as the archaeologist can tell us, began to emerge from the complexities of the social situation. All three owed much to favourable conditions in land, in stock, and above all in control of communications. Most prominent among the dynasties in 800 was the Danish house of Leire near Roskilde in Zealand. Carolingian pressure against Saxons and Frisians had brought Christendom to its doorstep. King Godfred (*c.* 800–810) provided a weighty answer to Frankish pride, and Danish pirates gave trouble to the emperor Charles the Great himself in his last years when border wars threatened the precarious Carolingian peace. An uneasy truce which laid the pattern of future development was established by the death of Charles the Great: on the Frankish side of the border special Marcher lordships were set up; on the Danish side great physical barriers in the form of defensive earthworks were built. As early as 808 Godfred himself had ordered his subordinate chieftains to construct the first version of the massive *Danevirke*, a great earthen rampart (much of which is still visible) across the foot of the Jutland peninsula from Slie fjord to the North Sea which was to serve as a protection against the Franks and their now conquered and subjected Saxon dependents. The dynasty of Godfred suffered a perilous period in the course of the 9th century. Attempts on the part of the missionary Anskar, based on his two centres of Hamburg and Bremen, to convert the Danes to Christianity were not successful though churches were set up (probably for the use primarily of Christian merchants) at Hedeby and Ribe – and at Birka in Sweden. Savage raiding from Denmark resulted in a spectacular sack of Hamburg in 845 and sporadic raiding throughout the century. At the most critical period of all, during the reign of King Alfred in England, 871–99, we are cruelly ill-informed about the domestic political situation in Denmark itself. Descendants of Godfred continued to be prominent in Danish and indeed in Frisian affairs throughout the greater part of the century, but it is impossible to establish the range, extent or nature of their so-called kingship. Two kings, Sigfred and Godfred, were killed in the disastrous campaign on the Dyle in 891, a victory that pointed the way to final recovery on the part of the East Frankish or German realm. Ohthere (a Norwegian sea-captain) and Wulfstan (possibly an Englishman), who gave King Alfred a graphic description of sea-voyages to the North and in the Baltic, are ambiguous and doubtful in their political references though clear enough about the continued integrity of the idea of Denmark as 'a geographical unit including Jutland and the islands together with the Danish territories in what is now Sweden, i.e. Skåne, but excluding Bornholm and Blekinge'.[4] But the end of the 9th century and the beginning of the tenth proved a period of political confusion which culminated with the submission of a large part of Denmark to the rule of Swedish kings.

In 800 the glory of the Swedish dynasty, the Ynglinga, lay in the past. Rich treasures from the Dark Ages have been found in the grave-mounds of old Uppsala. The kings who gave their name to the period, and the craftsmen who contributed the first Vendel goods flourished mightily in the 6th and 7th centuries A.D. The exploits of some of these kings of the Suear in the east-central plains of Sweden are hinted at in the English epic *Beowulf*. Many believe that the Swedes may have influenced directly the English dynasty of East Anglia. There was a period in the 7th and 8th centuries when the vigour of the dynasty expressed itself in external expansion. The big island of Öland lay under Swedish control. Gotland became an important Swedish centre. Clear evidence of early Viking settlement appears in Grabin in the Baltic lands. But the Swedish dynasty was in something of a backwater at the time the Viking Age opened, and it was not until the late 9th century or the initial decades of the tenth that Swedish kings emerged as an important force in internal Scandinavian politics when for a long generation (prompted probably by commercial motives) Swedish rulers governed the by now key settlement at Hedeby and a good portion of South Jutland.

Norway was as backward politically as Sweden in the early 9th century. The Westfold dynasty of the Ynglinga, centred around the district of modern Tonsberg, had emerged as the most powerful group, the men of the Vik, but their power had waned. It was not until the later years of the century, a generation after the first onslaught of Viking hordes, that the dynasty re-emerged triumphant. Their triumph is associated with the greatest name in early Norwegian history, that of Harold Fairhair. It is hard to disentangle the facts of his reign from the legendary accretions that have gathered around his name, but some things are clear. He was of the true Ynglinga line of the Westfold princes, the son of Halfdan the Black. He succeeded his father at an early age, probably in the 870s when he was still only 10. He had a very long reign which straddled the most creative generations of Viking political advance, died in 945, and was buried not in his native lands of the Oslo fjord but in Rogaland in south-west Norway. During his lifetime he established the idea if not always the practice of a unified Norwegian kingship. The men of the North, the Trondelag, recognised his overlordship. His massive contribution was made in the West, the focal point for so much of the Viking enterprise west over sea. Quite early in his reign, almost certainly between 885 and the end of the century, Harold won a tremendous sea victory at Hafrsfjord, not far from Stavanger, against a strong federacy of petty kinglets and jarls of the west and south-west. The victory was decisive in Harold's personal career and to some extent in Norway's history. Harold took to the south-west and the west (Hardanger, the orchard of Norway). He made it his favoured home, protected it from incursions back from dissident Vikings settled overseas, used it as his base for fierce punitive expeditions to the Scottish Isles, perhaps even to Ireland, and finally was buried there instead of in his ancestral home on the Oslo fjord. The men of the West were long to maintain their at times savage independence: to some considerable extent they do so still. But Harold deserves the traditional political credit ascribed to him for bringing the lands of the western fjords into close relationship with the lands and dynasty of the Vik.

It used to be the custom (particularly when the date of 872 was ascribed to the battle) to interpret Harold Fairhair's victory of Hafrsfjord as the true beginning of the full Viking Age. Many, including contemporaries, attributed the main force of the Viking onslaught, particularly the onslaught on England, to the dissastisfaction caused to active, turbulent young Scandinavian jarls and sea-captains by the discipline imposed by new and more effective kings. This view is no longer held. It was always difficult to reconcile with the known facts of the Danish situation, and even in a Norwegian context made only partial sense. It is more important to recognise Hafrsfjord as a step in the making of Norway, and to remember that the Viking outburst and the consolidation of the communities into larger kingdoms at home were contemporary and related processes.

If dissatisfaction and consolidation at home cannot be given pride of place in discussion of the reasons for the invasions, what are the possibilities facing the historian as he approaches this problem? Much will depend upon his own attitude to these affairs. The determinists who look always to impersonal large-scale movements outside the control of men, will tend to stress matters such as climate, the eternal pressure from the non-fertile to the fertile lands, and the timing of the maturity of certain techniques in agriculture, war and the mastery of movement on sea and on land. The more matter-of-fact historians who look to the particular and who stress the uniqueness of each situation and set of events will try rather to express the subtlety of the situation, the delicacy of the timing, and the element of chance involved in the success or non-success of particular movements and expeditions. Some stress the vigour and skill of the attackers: others the general fecklessness and incompetence of the defenders. Most tend to separate off the raids from the settlements, the problem of nature of attack from the problem of purpose of attack. Yet some themes emerge and re-emerge in all discussion of the reasons for the Viking invasion, and we shall start by approaching what might be termed the possible long-term reasons for this concerted move.

In the last generations, climate has received much attention from historians. The old certainty that climate in Western Europe had not changed significantly in historical times has been subject to criticism and to general erosion. Massive shifts have not, of course, occurred since the last Ice Age some 10,000 years ago, but it is now universally recognised that shifts of considerable significance have occurred in historic times, and are in fact still occurring. Weather and climatic fluctuations are taken seriously, for example, as factors to be considered in modern analysis of economic and demographic change in eighteenth- and nineteenth-century Scandinavia. Over a wider chronological range the working hypothesis of European climatologists is now largely based on the postulation of a post-Glacial climatic optimum in the fifth millennium B.C., a markedly colder and stormier climate from *c.* 1050–250 B.C., a secondary or 'little optimum' within the sub-Atlantic phase in the eleventh and twelfth centuries A.D. and a cold period of worsening climate in the later Middle Ages stretching into the early modern age and even earning for itself the name of a 'little Ice Age'.[5] The effects of this colder period, which seems to have reached a peak of severity about 1430 A.D., were dramatic on the Scandinavian world, especially on Iceland and on Greenland. Iceland's prosperity coincided with her existence as a free state (870–1262) and there was a steady decline in the later Middle Ages with a notable diminution in the amount of corn grown until it degenerated into a mere trickle by the sixteenth century. Worsening climatic conditions brought yet more disaster to Nordic Greenland, ending in the first half of the fourteenth century in the abandonment of the Western settlements, and at some point in the late fifteenth century in the Eastern settlements in their utter and irrevocable ruin. Attacks from Eskimoes following the drift ice south contributed to the disappearance of the Nordic Greenlanders as well as increasing difficulty in communication and sheer economic pressure in hard times on scanty resources.[6]

Knowledge of the difficulties faced by the men of the North in the fourteenth and fifteenth centuries at times led an earlier generation of scholars to suggest that a similar worsening of climate may have been a prime reason for the initial urge which sent the young Scandinavians on their Viking expeditions. This was by no means unreasonable. If progressive desiccation sent the Arabs north against the fertile crescent in the 7th century A.D., progressive gelidation might well be held to account for the Viking movement, south, west, and east in the 9th century. Unfortunately the evidence is heavily against such a hypothesis. The skills of the meteorologists, dendrochronologists, and students of ancient fauna and flora have established the Viking Age as on the whole a warm and dry period in the history of the north and west of Europe. Only for the period *c.* 860–*c.* 940, a vital period, it is true, for settlement in Britain and in Normandy, is there evidence for truly cold conditions in Scandidavia. Drift ice seems rarely to have been met south of 70°N in the tenth century, and was virtually unrecorded in these latitudes from 1020 to 1194. Mean temperature in northern waters was probably relatively high and pack ice may well have been confined to the central Arctic at latitudes of 80° or higher. Pressure from worsening climate cannot be accepted except as a contributory cause, modifying the nature of one specific phase of the Viking movement.[7]

Pressure of population on resources is quite a different matter, of course, and provides a serious background to the whole movement. But caution is necessary here in order not to exaggerate either the extent or the uniformity of such pressure and possible overpopulation. There is evidence that the population losses suffered in the 5th century A.D., had been made good by the end of the 9th, and possibly in some regions by a much earlier date. This had been brought about in part by immigration, but mostly by natural increase as the communities tightened their control of their initially isolated settlements. Immigration must not be overlooked. It is too easy to fall into the trap of seeing all folk-movement as one way only from the barbarous lands without the pale into the lands which had been part of the Roman Empire. In fact, the chaos of the folk-wandering brought about many reverse migrations, some from England back to Frankia and to Old Saxony in the 6th century A.D., some from the south and the false phantom of Italy and the Mediterranean back into the German heartlands and even further north. The Heruli appear to have re-established a settlement in the North in this period. An offshoot of the Burgundians, who gave their name to Bornholm, also probably immigrated into Scandinavia during these troubled times. However, natural increase, associated with a better mastery of farming conditions in the North under improving climatic conditions, is the most likely reason for a significant increase in population.

Yet this increase was not uniform throughout the Scandinavian lands. If we can trust the evidence of the historical written record it operated in a rather peculiar fashion. Denmark, potentially the most fruitful and fertile portion of Scandinavia, was something of a laggard. Sweden enjoyed only a partial intensification of rural activity and rural population – enough it is true to send its immigrants in to establish their fortress advance posts in the Eastern Baltic in the late 7th century. The best evidence comes, surprisingly enough, from Norway, and concerns directly, though on the northern fringe itself, the British Isles.

At some time in the 8th century there was a small but steady colonisation movement from the western fjords of Norway to the islands to the north and north-west of the Scottish mainland. Dating this movement is not easy, partly because it was continuous at least until the end of the tenth century. The basic problem of whether or not it was peaceful is not completely solved and probably varied considerably from group to group of islands. The culmination of the move came with the settlement of Iceland in the last 30 years or so of the 9th century. In our present state of knowledge the following conclusions seem acceptable about the nature and the chronology of the settlement of the groups of islands principally concerned. In the Orkneys, which had been a great centre of communication in Stone Age days, the Norwegians started their penetration *c.* 800 A.D., encountered a somewhat weak settlement of Picts and established a social and political dominance which converted the Orkneys into virtually a pure form of Norse society by the end of the century; attempts to plant themselves on the mainland, however, were substantially less successful and only a few isolated settlements were established in Caithness and Ross at this stage. In the Shetlands the evidence of Celtic settlements in depth is very weak, and it is possible that the Vikings found a decayed settlement with large tracts of potentially useful land unoccupied. Further to the north in the Faroes, initially in the early 9th century and in more intensity in the latter half of the century, the Norwegians settled in lands inhabited by only a few Celtic hermits. Iceland, the king-pin in Norwegian colonising history, was heavily settled, 870–930, with the help of strong elements, largely servile, from the Celtic world. To the west in the Hebrides matters were different, and here it appears that settlement was carried out with greater difficulty, with a much larger admixture of peoples, Celtic and Norse. More will be said in proper context of all these matters later in the volume. They need to be mentioned here as an important element in the earliest stages of Viking expansion, and as our best proof of some overpopulation and urge to find new lands in at least one part of the Scandinavian world. The need must have been great, it has been rightly held, to urge men and women and their families to attempt settlement on the bleak, windswept barren islands of the North Atlantic.

These early moves also give us a hint of two other factors in this story of early Viking expansion, one of which has received full and proper attention, while the other has been strangely neglected or underwritten: Scandinavian skill at boat-construction and Scandinavian technical skill at stock-breeding, notably the care and maintenance of sheep. No one who knows anything of the northern oceans will in any way belittle the first of these achievements. The Viking longship captures admiration by its sheer beauty. It is the end of a long line of trial and error in northern waters, leading from the rather crude rowing boats of the early Saxon immigrants to Britain, through the gradual evolution of the true keel and sailing ship of the late 7th century to the final flexible beauty of the Gokstad ship, as fine a creation as could be achieved, given the limitations of tools and materials available in the period. The less spectacular transport and trading vessels of the period, too, the knörrs, as they are commonly termed, were fine technical achievements. To arrive and to raid was one thing; to settle quite another. It is here that Norse and Celtic skill at animal husbandry must have come into its own. Such skills leave little trace; but without them the Scandinavian long, cautious, and highly successful occupation of the northern Isles of Britain, the Faroes and of Iceland itself, would have been impossible.

Much more trace, of course, has remained of the shipbuilding skill, and it is interesting to see how modern scholars turn to it time and time again in their search for reasons for the Viking outbursts. Their interest is sound. We know little of the reasons for achievement of technical excellence but can recognise the consequence when such technical excellence is achieved. The very nature of most of Scandinavia made the need for good water communications obvious. In the western fjords, for example, where communication to this day is mostly by water, communities could not exist in number until they had mastered the art of steady and reliable transport along the waterways. An odd feature of physical geography specially favoured the dweller in western Norway. The coastline itself along the whole massive length of the Norwegian coast is protected from the worst of the Atlantic gales by a series of islands which help to break to some extent the force of wind and tide. The great length of many of the fjords also helps to give protection and to calm the waters. The inner recesses of the Sogn and the Hardanger, to take two obvious examples, provide as splendid a training ground for builders and users of deep-water craft as can be found anywhere in the world. Time and some generations of peace were needed, but the skills once obtained were not lost until the need for them in turn disappeared in the modern world. Timber was in plentiful supply. The same ships which took peaceful colonisers to the Faroes could also carry young Viking thugs to attack monasteries and farms in peaceful Ireland and Northumbria.

Much work has been done recently on the detail of the technical achievements. It appears that the decisive moment of change came somewhere in the late 8th century. Ships earlier than that date, the Kvalsund ship, for example, were still predominantly rowing boats, capable of adaptation for sailing, but probably still of doubtful stability and incapable of continuous sailing for long stretches in Atlantic water. The maturing of the techniques of building ships with a heavy true keel and the development of methods of measuring the strakes more accurately and of keying in hull and ribs and deck more precisely ensured greater stability and flexibility. The late 8th and early 9th centuries was the period during which the art of the Scandinavian boat-builder was brought to a high point of perfection, and it is surely no coincidence that Viking activity originated during the same period. Trustworthy, easily manoeuvrable vessels, fast-moving and of shallow draught were indeed an essential and basic element in Viking movement and achievement.

Our best evidence comes from archaeological sources of a peculiarly dramatic kind, from the Viking ships miraculously preserved in the blue clay of the Oslo fjord, at Oseberg and particularly at Gokstad, and from the more recent and equally sensational finds made of sunken blockships (of the central Viking period) at Skuldelev in the Roskilde fjord. For earlier Viking technical achievement the evidence of the Gokstad ship stands supreme. In 1880 archaeologists discovered at Gokstad on the west side of the Oslo fjord, some 50 miles from Oslo itself, under a funerary mound, a fine ship, with fittings and grave goods, in an astonishing state of preservation. It was a sailing ship, nearly 80 feet long, $17\frac{1}{2}$ feet in breadth at its widest point, and some 6 foot, 5 inches from keel to gunwale at its maximum height. It was built substantially of oak, with only the decking, the mast, the yards and the oars of pine. The keel consisted of a single timber nearly 60 feet long, so substantial in fact that when a replica was built in 1892 the designers had to use Canadian oak for want of suitable straight solid oak timber in Scandinavia itself. The planking consisted of 16 strakes of varying thickness, most of them one inch thick but with extra breadth coming at the water-line (the tenth strake of $1\frac{3}{4}$ inches) and at the line of the oar-holes (the thirteenth strake of $1\frac{1}{4}$ inches). The fourteenth and fifteenth strakes were very thin (only $\frac{7}{12}$ inches) and were capped by a heavy gunwale of $4\frac{1}{4}$ inches by $3\frac{1}{2}$ inches. The hull was clinker built, and the ingenuity of the construction, notably the variation of thickness of the strakes, the spacing of the ribs and the keying-in of deck to hull, permitted maximum flexibility. The side-rudder, which extended 18 inches below the keel, permitted easy handling even in rough waters. The overall weight was $8\frac{1}{2}$ tons, or 10 tons fully laden. Oars were available for movement in shallow waters or in emergency. The replica built in 1892 crossed the Atlantic in less than a month in April 1893. Captain Magnus Andersen, who was in command, praised the ship for the elasticity and flexibility in handling which enabled it to reach speeds of over ten knots in relative comfort in spite of an unsophisticated rigging.

The Gokstad ship was the product of perhaps a century or a century and a half of experiment that finally enabled the Norsemen to command the northern seas. By 800 the technical knowledge needed to construct the longships and the more prosaic maid-of-all-work transports and traders had been acquired. All that was needed were men with the will and resources to direct their energies to the making of these magnificent instruments of movement, trade, and war.[8]

It would be wrong, however, to lay so much emphasis on the material achievement, the ships, to the neglect of the men who made them and the men who used them. Two further aspects of the Northerners' attainments and attitudes seem directly relevant to their activities in the late 8th and early 9th centuries. Skill in constructing ships is quite different from skill in navigation. How did the Scandinavians, and one thinks especially of the Norwegians in this respect, make the leap forward to face navigation across the open seas of the Atlantic and the North Sea? Later sagas tell of the existence of a sun-stone, a rudimentary compass, though information about such an instrument is vague and dubious. The calcite in the sun-stone permitted observations to be made of the sun's position even in sea mists, but more elaborate chronometric information was also needed of course before the information could be fully useful for navigation. Long experience and detailed knowledge of the stars and of the migration routes of birds are better attested and more obviously relevant to their early success. Detailed tables of the sun's midday latitude week by week throughout the year appear to have been known in tenth-century Iceland. A bearing-dial from twelfth-century Greenland suggests a quite sophisticated division of the navigation circle into 16 segments. With sufficient grasp of the apparent position of the midday sun (and of the Polar Star) effective mastery of vital information about the ship's latitude could be ensured. Norse sailing directions that survive are for the most part terse assessments of so many days' sailing on a direct reckoning.[9] It would be wrong and misleading to underestimate the weight of navigational aids and experience at the Norseman's disposal, but perhaps even more compelling than the existence of their technical navigational skills were the reasons, psychological and sociological why so many men were willing to invest their resources and to take the formidable risks involved in such journeyings. These were no ill-equipped hordes in fear of imminent starvation. What explanations can be offered of their attitudes? What did they seek from the outer world?

The answers that come most readily to mind are status, and the spoils of war: treasure, material possession and womenfolk. One possibility must be discussed, only to be dismissed as a serious explanation – national or religious pride. The Vikings were no *herrenvolk*; even less so were they missionaries. The recognised political leaders in Scandinavia were not Vikings. Only slowly did raiding and royal prestige become associated. The intense moves of the late 9th century might be read as reaction against the political consolidation attempted by rising kingship; they were certainly not a direct impulse towards consolidation of kingship. The initial Viking raids were joint-stock ventures, private, personal, and matters essentially for the young. Yet, of course, as we shall see, the release of so much energy and turbulence overseas gave the stay-at-home dynasties a wonderful opportunity. Parallels spring to mind with the Moslem world, though there a religion which prohibited fighting any fellow-believers played an important part. Parallels also exist, in a later more settled period, with the Norman world in the eleventh century when a similar release of turbulent aristocratic energy to Spain, to Italy, to England and on Crusade, helped both Norman dukes and French kings to build up permanent institutions of territorial government, though in that instance direct leadership of the movement by the Norman duke characterised and simplified the movement in the English direction.

Status is a difficult sociological concept, easy to recognise, hard to define. Possession of a free kindred, possession of land, and valour in war were the three principal sources of status in early Viking times. In this respect several possibilities emerge as worthy of enquiry in relation to the motives which sent so many young men a-Viking. Overpopulation in the absolute sense may not have been a decisive factor, except in the hard and barren lands of western Norway. Overpopulation in selected classes of society is a very different matter. When we first glimpse the land-law of the North, we find that odal-right, while making ample provision for the eldest son, contrasts vigorously with a system of primogeniture. Every son had his right in the parental homestead. Survival of even three sons from each family could therefore lead to dislocation and social peril for the family group. What evidence we have suggests that the Vikings were adequately prolific. It is reasonable to suppose that the settled middle rung of free farmer bred more children more successfully than other groups: the Scandinavian social system favoured such groups. It would need only a very few settled generations to bring about a state of affairs where the three status factors mentioned above, freedom, land, and opportunity to show and benefit from valour were gravely disturbed. Young sons, or sons more mobile by temperament would look elsewhere, away from the land, for their status achievements.

There remains the question of bravery, valour in war. The Vikings are known by universal reputation as a turbulent crew, not inhibited in any way from internecine warfare. Universal reputation does not always reflect universal truth, and we must not be too misled by lurid stories from saga and poetry, stories chosen often because of their exceptional nature. The Vikings had their own standards. Again, matters of timing, of pure chronology, become very important. Given two or three generations of prosperous farming a network of kindred relationships would be built up over so wide an area that immediate achievement of military prestige would not easily be acquired. Tests of manly strength would result in bootless crimes or wasteful feuds. Quarrels between the more consolidated groups, the men of the Frostathing and the men of the Gulathing, or between Geats and Swedes offered some scope; but these men were basically of the same tongue and type. War overseas was more adventurous and in the initial stages at least much more profitable. Status, difficult to obtain territorially, could be obtained by war, and especially by war overseas. As the young men discovered that status and profit were multiplied a hundred-fold when they turned their aggressive instincts away from their fellow and relatively impoverished Norsemen to the fat lands and monasteries overseas, so did the feeling of solidarity among the Norsemen increase and intensify. Nothing brings human groups together so closely as a shared successful enterprise. Internecine warfare remained a feature and a disgrace to Norse society. To draw the comparison again with the Mohammedan world, not even the sternest strictures of a new world religion could keep the Moslem world from savage internal warfare for more than a generation. But the first generation could be vital: the back of the defensive systems protecting the southern arc of the fertile crescent was broken in the first generation after Mahomet's death (632–60) and before civil war racked the new Mohammedan world. On a smaller scale in northern waters the second half of the 9th century represented a corresponding period. The difference came, and it is a difference explicable by scale, techniques and scope with the further half a century and more of probing, exploratory raids that preceded the decisive generations.

Both status and bravery were naturally closely associated with the spoils of war, sheer loot from piracy. Precious goods, slaves, men and women, all the proceeds of a material civilisation greater than their own, acted as a bait and as a spur for Viking ventures. Yet even this simple proposition is not as simple as it seems. Loot was and remained an incentive as late as the eleventh century. But it was often associated with other forms of gain which serve as a reminder of the complexity of this phase in human history. It is not too difficult, and it is sometimes profitable, to analyse the types of Viking adventurer into the categories of pirate, coloniser, and trader. Differences of emphasis at least, touching on one or other of these categories, can be attributed to the careers of most of the men we study. The categories are, however, rarely exclusive. The same men could be pirates one day, colonisers the next, and peaceful traders again the third. Instances can be multiplied, even in the high Viking period, of ships' crews setting off jauntily, uncertain whether to trade or loot. Many of the most successful chieftains and sea-captains were opportunists of the first order, as ready to turn an honest as a dishonest penny, if the opposition to piracy looked too dangerous. Coolness of judgement and an ability to gauge the odds was as characteristic of the successful Viking chief as his legendary bravery and audacity. Nor must we forget that the colonisation enterprises, rightly praised, in the northern islands and indeed over large sections of Britain and part of Normandy, were not matters for small family units of freemen working in isolation. In the North land was won by hard toil against savage climatic conditions. Slave labour was a much to be desired asset. Our best information comes from Iceland and there, as we know, from the great record of the land-taking which has remained from the period 870–930, Celtic thralls were a feature of this earliest stage in settlement. Indeed some of the credit which, as has been mentioned earlier, goes rightly to the Norseman for this animal husbandry should in equity be shared by their Celtic slaves, from time immemorial associated with the shepherd's craft. Social historians stress the importance to the economy of this early period of the intelligent use of summer pasturage at shielings often quite remote from the main farm; the Celtic word -arg (argh) is frequently found in northern place-names (*ærgi*, for example, is Faroese) to describe such shielings. The elegiac lament of the modern Welsh poet may well have sounded over Faroe fell and Icelandic dale.

> *O God, why makest thou the Vale of Aurland so beautiful*
> *And the life of an old shepherd so short?*

While Celtic shepherds and Irish princesses are to be found, the ones on the farms and the other in the genealogies of many Icelandic freeholders, the need for servile labour was no less to his kinsman further south, in Ireland, Northumbria, Eastern Mercia or the Cotentin. Here the fight was against man rather than nature. Freedom among the small landowners remained a characteristic of Scandinavianised north-western Europe, but so did thraldom. Even after settlement the incentive for successful slave-raiding was not removed.

More important perhaps than the slaving and sheer garnering of loot was the association with relatively peaceful trading. This aspect of Viking life is only just beginning to receive its proper due in connection with the reason for the outbreak. In Roman times Scandinavia may have been something of a backwater but it was by no means an unknown backwater. In particular knowledge of the amber-bearing qualities of the Baltic was commonplace to the Romans, and a well-beaten route extended from the Empire through Denmark to the lands known historically as East Prussia and Lithuania. No regular trade route existed in the 6th and 7th centuries: the times were not propitious. But in the 8th we have the beginnings of firm evidence of revived contact. Within Scandinavia itself three areas emerged as settlements through which contact with the Christian world could be effected. In modern-day Sweden the townships of Birka on the great lake Mälar gave their first sign of organised trading life about this period. In Norway the archaeologist has found at *Skiringssalr* (to the south of the western shore of the Oslo fjord) evidence of trading that may well go back to the earliest period. Denmark, of immense importance in this respect in the 9th century, is a more difficult case. Hedeby, at the head of Slie fjord in modern Schleswig, presents special problems. Some traders may have been active as early as the late 8th century: military and political endeavour are more characteristic of the scanty records which remain. It is no accident that the three trading centres are all associated with areas that later come to be important dynastic headquarters. This was a matter for the future: the joint growth (and mutual advantage gained by proximity) of kingship and honest trade was a matter of general moment in the history of Western Europe. For our purpose, the isolation of reasons for the Viking outburst, it is sufficient to mention the fact that the revival of regular trade, with all that implies in the way of knowledge of routes and resources appears to have occurred at roughly the same period as the earlier Viking attacks. The tangled web of trade and piracy continued to spread through the Viking period. We remember the Norseman as a founder of fortified markets as well as a despoiler of churches.

Contemporaries, puzzled and fearful, attempted also to isolate the reasons for these savage attacks from the North. Many dismissed them as an act of God. The record-makers were Christian and churchmen, and it is natural that they should talk in terms of a heathen scourge. Indeed it is often pointed out that our picture of

Vikings are at times highly coloured because so much of their energy was directed against a church they had no reason to respect and whose goods they coveted. No wonder the clerical historians talked of spring fertility rites and polygamy which to their minds led straight to problems of overpopulation. Undoubtedly, too, the speed and mobility of the attacks led to a further strengthening of the view that here was indeed a heathen visitation brought about because of the sins of the people. The Northern capacity for long continuous journeying and for long campaigns remained a mystery to the more settled folk of the West. None of the voyaging, except to Greenland and Vinland and around the North Cape, was completely new to Western experience. It was the knitting together of known short routes into a long continuous and almost routine whole that rightly impressed the Western world. The supernatural element did not altogether wear off, even after longer acquaintance. Their language was intelligible at least to the English and to the continental German. Their religious and some of their social customs were not. They came into Western experience at a very odd moment in the life of the Western world. Ideas of a larger unity in the Carolingian world were deeply tinged with religious thought: Christendom not Europe was the general conception behind advanced political thought. Charles the Great had been crowned and the Empire formed that the heathen might not mock the Christian. Not mockery but butchery, robbery, and deep affliction was the fate of much of this new-found Christendom at the hands of these heathen invaders.

To this point we have looked largely at the inner life of the Scandinavian world to find reasons for the Viking outburst. In conclusion it is necessary to look briefly again at the peoples they attacked. Some political cause of their success, as has already been suggested can be found in the very nature of the formation of the Carolingian Empire. Destruction of Frisian sea-power, in particular, made the way easier for Viking seafarers. More important still is the simple fact of disunity underlying the new imperial fabric. Economic resources would not permit unitary government to be sustained over so large an area. Squabbles, and senseless feuding of successor princes, gave the Scandinavians ever-increasing scope for action. Britain lay on the fringe, open to the North. Some of the same inadequacies that applied to the Carolingian Empire applied also to her political structure. It is with the British polity that our next chapter will be chiefly concerned.

2.

Britain at the Beginning of the Scandinavian Invasions

M. Lucien Musset, when he chose a sub-title for his short but classic exposition of the barbarian invasions of the 7th, 8th and 9th centuries, rightly referred to the 'Second Assault against Christian Europe' – as opposed to the earlier Moslem attacks.[1] This title gives much of the right flavour to the period. Avars, Slavs, and above all the Magyars were in their moments of attack aggressively non-Christian. Conversion and slackening of onslaught arrived together. The triumph of cross over hammer marks the end of the Viking Age.

In the first instance, however, religion had little to do with the enterprise. Wealth and political weakness were more obvious spurs to attack. It is indeed notable, not only with the Vikings, but more so with the Magyars, how raids slackened as they grew more dangerous and less profitable. The feudal lord and the rudimentary castle checked the barbarian onslaught.

Of all areas of Western Europe, Britain endured most and suffered most. In order to see why this should have been we must look more closely at the situation inside Britain itself about 800 A.D. Geographical factors, sheer proximity to sea-raiders capable of taking the North Sea in their stride, were decisive in one sense, but the full picture cannot be seen unless we grasp the economic and political state of Britain at the time of the opening of the attacks.

It is wrong to think exclusively in political terms. Britain was, it is true, heavily divided into many political and ethnic groups, each under its own king or kings, Saxon, Briton, Scot, or Pict. But there was common ground as well among the inhabitants of Britain. By 800 A.D. they were all Christian and, to judge from surviving records, quite deeply so. At the Synod of Whitby in 663 a decision was taken whereby in matters affecting the dating of Easter, baptism, and the tonsure of monks, Roman practice rather than the indigenous Celtic forms would be observed. Gradually the native Celtic communities followed the Northumbrian example. Rome became dominant in polity as well as custom. Free intercourse was achieved between Celtic and Germanic missionaries. The Celts, and particularly the Irish, became famous throughout Europe, and above all in the well-beaten paths that lay through the monastic houses of St Gall and of Bobbio on the way to Rome. English missionaries concentrated more on the continental German lands. The greatest of their number, Boniface, Winfrith of Crediton in Devon, martyred by the Frisians in 755, is rightly known as the Apostle of the Germans. Britain remained outside the political structure of the Carolingian Empire. Her men, Irish, Saxon, Welsh, and Scottish were deep in the heart of the Christian church, a most active and dynamic element in the ecclesiastical and spiritual life of Western Christendom.

A similar coincidence of aim and achievement among the communities of Britain can be found in the artistic field. The late 7th century had seen the blossoming of a fine cultural movement into what is often termed the Northumbrian Renaissance. New vitality and intensity of artistic experience was reflected in the finest products of the age, the Northumbrian gospel-books of which the Lindisfarne Gospels, the Book of Durrow, and the Book of Kells give us our finest extant examples. Stone crosses, fine sculpture, and skill in church building also indicate the strength of the artistry of the period. Nor were the literary arts neglected. In the person of Bede, theologian, historian, and scientist, Northumbrian produced the outstanding literary figure of his age. This renaissance was no mere sudden flaring-up of cultural activity with no future to it. The 8th century was a very troubled century politically. Church life was disrupted, and evidence of some corruption and falling-off in standards is easy to find. But the main stream of cultural and literary life remained powerful. Archbishop Egbert's school and library at York were among the best known in Christendom. The outstanding scholar at the court of Charles the Great, Alcuin, later abbot of Tours, had been trained at that school. From the Celtic world Irish scholars continued their fabled peregrination, carrying with them their typical flair for ascetic observance and scholarly extravagance. Hisperic Latin was the badge of their origins, and pride of their schools. Diversity existed in obvious and manifold ways in Britain. It is well to remember the other side of the medal, the common religion, the common observance, the common and joint cultural activity, and the high reputation enjoyed by British scholars and monks throughout Christendom.

In the economic field it is much harder to generalise. One huge point of contrast existed in the 8th century as in previous ages as far back as human record can go: the contrast between highland and lowland. All the communities of these islands had by the end of the 9th century long emerged from the nomadic stage. They were settled peoples, drawing their sustenance from the lands they tilled and the herds and flocks they maintained. They were eaters of meat and bread, the sheep and the cow providing the staple meat diet, oats and barley rather than wheat the staple cereal diet. The differences came in emphasis, imposed by the nature of the land and the weather. The Anglo-Saxons predominated in the drier flatter lands of the south and east; their cereal output was greater. The Celtic peoples dwelt in the more mountainous and wetter west; the herdsman rather than the ploughman remained the dominant figure in their economy. This simple distinction, one of emphasis, it must be stressed, is of vast importance when we consider differences in social organisation. Cereal-growers had a better chance of storing a surplus. Stronger royal authority and a stronger territorial church could and did thrive upon such a surplus. Tribal institutions persist longer in communities where a man's wealth is reckoned in cattle and sheep. The plough and a money economy have close and intimate associations.

It is probably no mere accident that the main political division in Britain, between Germanic and Celtic, came roughly along this line of division. Our records of the English settlement of England tend to be connected with epic military incidents, the exploits of a Ceawlin or a Centwine, the strength of a Penda, or the victories of Oswy. As the work of the archaeologist and the place-name expert grows more precise, so too does the realisation grow stronger that these selected glamorous careers or incidents are only history's shorthand. An unrecorded movement of settlers and colonisers often preceded political action. If we take one obvious example, the expansion of the West Saxon to the borders of Devon and Cornwall, the pure political record would have us believe that the conquest of Devon was the special achievement of King Ine (688–725); but no one would deny the presence of large numbers of Saxon settlers in Devon at least one whole generation before the reign of Ine. The Saxon advance halted when the supply of good arable for villages and open-fields gave out. Land predominant for the plough, was as much an economic, social, and incidentally a racial, bounty for the German in the north-west as the date-palm was for the Arab in the south.

An obvious, and yet curiously neglected, difference between the

Germanic and Celtic settlers in Britain needs some comment at this point. The Celts knew no coins; theirs was no money economy. The English by contrast knew coins – that true index of the ploughman and the trader – from the early years of the 7th century. Close proximity to the gold-loving Merovingian world, the stimulus given to renewed continental traffic to Frankia and to Rome by the conversion of the heathen English to Christianity in the 7th century: these had their part to play. But it would be wrong to place too much weight on the social and ecclesiastical side. Some of the exotic coinage, the gold *solidi* struck at the London mint, the free circulation of Merovingian *solidi* and *tremisses*, can be attributed to the church or to the royal courts stimulated by the church. But from the late 7th century through to the end of the 8th there occurred a development of the greatest significance in the life of the English communities. A silver coinage of increasingly fine quality was struck by the native kings. In the first instance this coinage consisting of rather thick and often ugly silver pieces sometimes known as *sceattas* but more strictly early pennies, was rather a trader's coinage, based on Frisian types, running essentially in a southern *Nordseekreis*. In Northumbria a somewhat coarse coinage continued to predominate well into the 9th century. But in England south of the Humber, and especially in the last generation of the 8th century, the silversmiths under royal authority started to produce coins of quite startlingly high quality, coins moreover that were to remain with only relatively small modification the dominant coins in England during the following 500 years. The penny, the exquisite silver penny which was to set England on her course as a trading nation, was the product of this century of strain and strife. At first in Kent under sub-kings, and then more extensively from mints at Canterbury and London under the control of Offa, king of the Mercians (757–96) the penny became the current coin of the realm. It was struck in the royal name: *Offa rex* was the common inscription on the obverse. On the reverse was the name of the moneyer, but not yet, as became the custom later, the name of the mint. A few gold coins were also struck, probably for ceremonial purposes; one – a gold dinar imitated from the Moslem currency but bearing the name *Offa rex* – was found at Rome. Their importance was secondary. The existence of a sound silver currency is the economic fact of prime importance, a vital clue to the economic advance and potential of the English lords, and a pointer to the contrast in economic development between England and the coinless Celtic lands of this period.[2]

But, of course, as we know, the Scandinavians with their massive gifts for adaptation and assimilation were equally at home in both these economic milieus. It is amusing but wickedly unhistorical to consider what might have happened if they had not intervened in British history. Larger groups, national groups, would without doubt have formed: the beginnings of such formation were already apparent long before 800. Would the groups have coalesced along more rigid linguistic and racial lines, had the Scandinavians not been present as the catalyst in this crucible of nations? Would the England of the Middle Ages have stretched to Edinburgh and the Wales to Dumbarton, with Scottish Ireland embracing Albany and the Picts expanding north from their Caledonian fortress to colonise yet more deeply the Isles? A delicious fantasy, no doubt, but historically a nonsense. Geography alone, given the economic resources of the times, would have imposed a barrier on a kingdom that stretched from St David's to Dumbarton; and strained the resource of a kingship that ran from Canterbury to Edinburgh. Yet it is good to remember that the nations as we come to know them were not god-given inevitable entities. And it is good to reflect that the Scandinavians played a part, possibly a decisive part, in the making of England, of Scotland, of Ireland, and of Wales.

The division into four nations, still not inevitable but foreshadowed, gives a convenient basis for discussion of the political state of Britain in the late 8th century. England with its greater economic resources had undoubtedly progressed furthest along the path to strong kingship and political unity. The leading dynasty was that of the Mercian peoples and the outstanding figure Offa, 757–96, king of Mercia and effective head of a confederation of Germanic peoples south of the Humber. He was very much a military chieftain, but he was also more than that. His court, the heart of which consisted of Mercian noblemen, was attended by clerics from all over England. His effective authority ran from the Channel to the Humber. The boundary with the Celt in the south-west ran to the Tamar and the present line of division between Devon and Cornwall. His finest achievement, which still bears his name, was the establishment of an agreed boundary with the Welsh along the line of Offa's dyke, known as *Clawdd Offa* to the Welsh. This boundary was often violated: it did not follow a strict linguistic line nor did it remain inflexible. But its general success, legal and physical, in limiting the spheres of interest of the English and the Welsh should on no account be underestimated: its construction was a political and diplomatic act of the first importance for the age. North of the Humber Offa attempted no more than punitive expeditions and marriage alliances: his interests and the achievements by which he should be judged lay to the south. His coinage, his style, *rex Anglorum*, his charters, and

35

his courts mark him out as one who made great contributions to the future unity of England.[3]

There were, of course, imperfections in the Mercian polity. The facts and nature of Anglo-Saxon settlement, the limited though growing resources of the new communities, and geographical and political peculiarities, led to the creation of a multiplicity of small kingdoms which were only slowly whittled down in number. Mercian success came to be bitterly resented in Kent, smarting under harsh military repression and furious at the temporary elevation of Lichfield into an archbishopric, an affront to the dignity of Canterbury. East Anglia was given even deeper cause for hatred by the political murder at the instigation of Offa of the young king Ethelbert, late in Offa's reign. Wessex was restive, with its most promising young prince Egbert driven into exile at the court of Charles the Great. England was not yet half-made. The efforts of a new dynasty, that of Egbert and his successors in Wessex, would be fully exercised in the 9th century to exploit these themes of unity part developed by the Mercians. The greatest of these successors, Egbert's grandson Alfred who ruled the West Saxon kingdom from 871 to 899, in the vastly different context of the late 9th century, advanced the making of England to a yet further stage. But by that time the themes of unity and of Scandinavian invasion were inextricably tangled.

There remains, before we leave the English communities, the very complex problem of the lands to the north of the Humber. In the second half of the 7th century Northumbria appeared to be the dominant power among the Anglo-Saxon kingdoms. After the defeat and death of the Mercian Penda in 655, Oswy, triumphant in his military and religious enterprises – he had presided at the Synod of Whitby – seemed indeed a true Bretwalda. But the defeat of his successor Ecgfrith at the battle of Nechtansmere in 685 at the hands of the Picts proved a symbolic event. For the succeeding century the political history of Northumbria provides one of the most dismal episodes in the whole of English history. Ravages from outside, from the Picts in the north and from the Mercians in the south, were made worse by internal divisions and dissensions. The kingdom had developed from two different centres, along two different lines, and under the direction of two different dynasties, both of which however claimed descent from a 6th-century warrior, Icel, himself a descendant of Woden. The more prosperous section lay to the south, the old kingdom of Deira, with York as its centre and the fertile vale of York as its cereal-bearing economic heart. To the north, from the Tyne to the Forth was the ancient kingdom of Bernicia with the gaunt rock of Bamborough its centre. Deira was more Germanic, Bernicia more of a mixture. Deira relied more on arable: Bernicia on arable and fine sheep-pasture – though the crop-raising lands of the East Lothian are neglected at peril. Natural geographical and economic contrasts between these two constituent parts of the Northumbria kingdom were heightened by savage, insensate, feuding in the royal dynasties. Even in the 7th century this was apparent. In the 8th century matters grew worse, royal blood offered no protection, and most of the rulers of Northumbria between 708 and 800 died of violence. Yet, such is the complexity of the social fabric, the church continued to flourish in Northumbria, at York, and especially at Bede's old home (673–735), the joint monastery of Jarrow–Wearmouth. The combination of still wealthy monasteries and disrupted kingship created a favourable stamping-ground for Norse raiders: it was no accident that the most powerful of the early blows fell on Lindisfarne.

The disruption of the Northumbria kingdom undoubtedly contributed greatly to (just as it was in a sense the product of) Mercian success further south. In similar fashion northern politics were also greatly affected by this period of Northumbrian turbulence and weakness. Scotland as we know it did not then exist. There were no hard and fast political boundaries in North Britain. At the same time, by 800 there were fairly clearly defined settlement and linguistic patterns and the main racial mixture that was to make up the medieval kingdom of Scotland – with the conspicuous exception of the Scandinavian element itself – was already to be found north of the Tweed.

To begin with there was a very strong English element, northern Bernicia, the Northumbrians dwelling to the north of the Cheviots. Under sheer pressure of political events this was drawn more and more into the orbit of the northern kings, seeking its protection from Dumbarton or Stirling rather than from Bamborough or York. A legal concession of this area, of Lothian, was made by one of the greatest of English kings, Edgar, probably after his coronation in 973, and certainly no earlier than 971. This was a politic and sensible move on the English king's part, acknowledging the military strength of the Scottish king, Kenneth II, in return for Kenneth's recognition of Edgar's overlordship. Kenneth II was sent back to his own country with great honour, and was probably given estates in England at this time to sustain him and his successors on their visits south to the English court. The resulting peace was used by English kings with some success and Lothian itself was temporarily recovered by the Northumbrian earls late in the tenth or early in the eleventh century. However the defeat of a Northumbrian army at Carham in 1018 finally confirmed the concession, and rounded off the political structure of Scotland as we know it.

Concentration on the affairs of Northumbria and Lothian anticipates events. We need to look back to the Celtic world, to see how Celtic Scotland was shaping in the 8th century. The people who were to give their name to Scotland, the Scots themselves, were only one among the three principal groups of Celtic settlers in the North. Their origins lay across the Irish Sea in Ireland. In the difficult days of the 4th and 5th centuries they crossed to the islands and then to the mainland north of the Clyde. Winning an unenviable reputation for themselves for ferocity and piracy they established their kingdom in modern Argyll, in the province which Bede knew as Dalriada (an echo in name of the province of Dalriada in Northern Ireland). They had never been subject to Rome. Their speech was Celtic, Q-Celtic or Goidelic Celtic: that is to say the branch of the Celtic tongue which retained (to mention a conspicuous characteristic) the sound -k- initially in words like *Can* (head) or *cadair* (four) where the other main branches modified the sound to -p- (*Pen, pedwar,* in modern Welsh). By *c.* 800 the Scots had effective control of most of the lands from the Moray Firth to the isles of Jura, Islay and the peninsula of Kintyre, from the kingdom of Fife to Glasgow. They had been Christianised in the 5th and 6th centuries: St Kentigern and St Columba were their great religious figures. The holy island of Iona was their principal religious centre. Their language was to dominate most of the north and the west of historic Scotland.

Closely associated with them throughout the whole of the period were the most mysterious of all the peoples of these islands, the Picts. It is not even certain that they were Celtic people, though general opinion, acting on the pitifully few scraps of information that can be gleaned from fossilised place-name forms, from the material remains, from the picture-stones of Pictland, and from outside references, now favours strongly Celtic origins for at least the ruling groups among the Picts. The dominant language was a Brythonic dialect, possibly with closer affinities to Gaulish Celtic rather than to Cumbrian or Welsh. The possibility of the late survival of an indigenous Bronze Age non-Indo-European speaking element among the historic Picts is perhaps the most compelling of the various hypotheses that have been advanced to explain the peculiarities of these people, uncommunicative and yet fertile in artistry. The name Picts, the painted men, was given to them by the Romans, applied to all those who dwelt to the north of the narrow neck of Scotland from the estuary of the Clyde to the Firth of Forth. Christianity reached them from the ministries of St Ninian in the late Roman period, but it is now generally held that the results of this British mission were not as deep and permanent as used to be thought. Pictish tribes were diverse and heterogeneous, and it is only after the emergence of more recognisable historic kings in the middle of the 6th century that the task of permanent conversion to Christianity took place under the direction of Irish missions led by St Columba. Politically the Picts had been subject to heavy pressure from the British peoples of Strathclyde. The arrival of immigrant Scots into Argyll, with whom they were initially at least often in alliance, further restricted their activities. Northumbrian expansion to the north in the 7th century (Edinburgh was in English hands from 638) was checked, as we have seen, after the Pictish victory at Nechtansmere in 685. Roman Christian observances were adopted by the Picts in the second decade of the 8th century. By 800 they were however essentially men of the north-east, Caledonians and islanders. They had their own customs, including a system of succession to the kingdom through females which later passed for several centuries into Scottish practice. In 843 under the Scottish king, Kenneth MacAlpin, Picts and Scots were brought together in what was to prove an enduring political union. The new Scottish/Pictish kingdom was sometimes known as Scotland but more often, from its ancient Roman designation, as Albany.

The third and last of the Celtic groups of Scotland is different again from the other two. In the south-west of the kingdom the political position was confused to the point of bewilderment in the centuries which followed the collapse of Roman military power in Britain. A mixed but predominantly Romano-British population straddled the Wall, and achieved some sort of political shape from the effects of a succession of federate chiefs. These peoples, living in the modern shires of North Lancashire, Westmorland, Cumberland, Dumfries and Ayrshire, extended over an area known by the two territorial designations of Cumbria and Strathclyde. Under Northumbrian pressure in the 7th century most of Cumbria passed under Anglo-Saxon domination, though retaining its essentially Celtic population and at times turning for political leadership to the north, to Traprain Law and *Alclut*. Scandinavian pressure in raids and in settlement had a tremendous impact on the southern (English) part of this area. In 945 Edmund of England ceded all of Cumbria to King Malcolm I of Albany, a great-grandson of Kenneth MacAlpin, in return for a promise of support by sea and by land. It is unlikely that this cession involved territory to the south of the Wall but was

39

meant to apply to Strathclyde. Within the following three-quarters of a century the hold of the Scottish king was strengthened in Strathclyde and with the further gains made in Lothian the shape of the mainland kingdom of Scotland became fully visible.[4]

There remain the islands but their story is so complicated and so intimately enmeshed with our Scandinavian ventures that it is best treated in detail in an account of the invasions themselves. It is sufficient in this context to note that a whole range of islands, Shetlands, Fair Isle, Orkney, and some of the mainland in the modern shires of Caithness, Ross, Cromarty, and Sutherland, fell under Scandinavian control and were colonised mostly by men of Norwegian origin. Further west in the Hebrides, and in a range of island settlements again as far south as the Isle of Man, the Vikings settled in large numbers and came in some areas to predominate in institution and in language: in other areas, some of which are Gaelic speaking to this day, they became no more than a formidable minority group. Their settlements, particularly those in Orkney and the Isle of Man constituted strategic centres of the greatest importance, bases and recruiting grounds for sea-raiders whose mobility by sea was their greatest single asset.

Mention of the Isle of Man, that stepping-stone in the middle of the Irish Sea, leads naturally to discussion of the last of the big political units of the Celtic World, to Wales and to Ireland itself. Behind Offa's dyke in Wales political groups were also sorting themselves out into familiar historical shapes. In the latter half of the 7th and 8th centuries there were, it is true, no kings or princes of the status of Maelgwn Gwynedd, Cadwallon or Cadwalladr in earlier generations. The church retained its importance but not as a Romanic unifying force in any way. The political successes of the age seem to have been made at the local level with the establishment of more or less permanent divisions of spheres of influence, the cantrefs of historic Wales. The four principal units of varying importance and integrity remained the kingdoms of Deheubarth (from modern Pembroke to Brecon) and Morgannwg in the south, of Powys (desperately overshadowed by Mercian military might) in the north-east, and Gwynedd in the north-west. Only in Gwynedd in the early 9th century are there signs of promise of larger scale and more permanent royal institutions. Under Merfyn Frych (the Freckled) 825–44, something of a cosmopolitan culture developed, fed no doubt by the wealth of the granaries of Anglesey. In the event, as we shall see, the strength of his new dynasty coupled with the toughness of local institutional life was to serve Wales well during the period of Viking irruption.

Ireland at the end of the 8th century was in a precarious political state. Its isolation and the migrations to Scotland had left it in a somewhat underpopulated condition. Agriculture was at a more backward level than elsewhere in the British Isles, and it was only as stockraisers that the Irish had a good reputation. Their equable and damp climate was then, as later, their greatest economic asset, ensuring as it did an abundance of good pasture. One feature of Irish life stood as altogether conspicuous and noteworthy in its age: the religious. Nowhere had Christian missionaries been so successful as in Ireland. During the Roman occupation of Britain Ireland had been outside the pale and it was not until the decline of Romania that Christianity reached the Irish shores. The mission of St Patrick in the early 5th century was reinforced in the succeeding two centuries by the very turbulence of this age of migration. Christianity early received a peculiar ascetic twist in Irish society. The dominant element in the polity became not the ordered territorial diocese subject to a bishop as elsewhere in the Christian Roman world. Ireland knew no *civitates* to secure a basis for such ecclesiastical divisions, and instead the monastery, governed by an abbot who was often a prominent tribal figure, became the typical unit in the Irish church. The Irish monks were not however necessarily bound to the cloister. Very full play was given to the individual. Within the community the ascetic ideal was that of the hermit within his cell. Austerities often matched in their extremes the wildness and extremes of nature in which the early monasteries were planted: the rocky fortresses off the west Irish coast or the windswept banks of the northern lochs. Missionary enterprise was also actively encouraged, no doubt as one among the austere practices that signalled salvation. In the 6th century Irish enterprise concentrated on the North: their chief work lay among the Picts and the Scots. Contact was also re-established with the Continent. Irish monks were prominent on the road to Rome, setting up their homes at Bobbio and Luxeuil and gaining an enviable reputation as teachers and students. The 7th century saw the culminating point in their work. From Iona through Lindisfarne they provided an important, and many would say the most important, element in the conversion in depth of the pagan Anglo-Saxons. Roman discipline and organisation gave the church in England its characteristic shape and order. Without Irish manpower it is hard to see how in the 7th century the conversion could have been achieved so successfully and peacefully in depth. At the end of the 7th century the Northumbrian renaissance owed much to Irish influence and example.

All these achievements, in the mission field and in the cultural field, reacted upon the church in Ireland itself. Awareness of fellowship in great enterprise served as something of a social bond to the Irish. The nature of the enterprises drew the Irish away from political success. The abbeys flourished but native kingship decayed. Tribal institutions persisted, but loyalties were attracted more to the great tribal monasteries rather than to the royal courts. Such strivings as there were towards larger political units were if not negligible at least restrained. A rough division was apparent between the north, including much of the west and centre, or the kingdom of Connaught, and the southern kingdom of Leinster, but men's natural loyalties passed (as in Wales) to the smaller groups, that can still be identified in place-names, into the men of Fermanagh, Monaghan, Armagh, Tyrone, or Derry. In such situations quarrels, sheep-stealing, cattle-raiding, and feuds over marriage arrangements were endemic. But, as far as we can see from the scanty and patchy records, the quarrels lacked the ferocity which characterised, for example, the Mercian campaigns against Kent or the Northumbrian civil wars of the same period. The wealth of the church, in spite of the closeness of tie between tribe and monastery, remained relatively untouched. It was not until the Viking rulers showed the way that the native Irish princes joined in, to make the 9th century one of the unhappiest in Ireland's history.[5]

Political disunity and instability might well therefore have made Ireland a tempting prize for Viking enterprise. Yet awareness of the unity of the island was not completely lost and even received some institutional expression. Authority and physical power rested in the smaller units, but the concept of an *ard-ri*, a high king, persisted, and was given some air of reality by the reconnection of a ruling line in the persons of the descendants of Niall of the Nine Hostages, a high king who flourished at the end of the 4th and beginning of the 5th centuries. The position of *ard-ri* was held by men claiming descent from Niall from the early 5th century to the opening years of the eleventh century. From 734 the northern and southern branches of the family enjoyed the honour in alternate succession. But only towards the end of the period did the high-kingship begin to indicate, let alone realise, its potentialities.

This rapid survey of the political state of the British Isles has been made with the object of showing how open the communities were to vigorous campaigning from outside. Only the English with their arable wealth had made serious strides towards unity, and there the sheer military weight of the Mercian house was breeding its own resistance. The Viking impact in its way forced unity upon the four main communities, but the shape of the political units in which the

English, the Welsh, the Irish and the Scots would respectively predominate was by no means predetermined. Distortions, variations,
peculiarities in what a racial or economic determinist would call the
normal pattern abound. The direct reason for such so-called aber-
rations may often be attributed to the Norseman.

3.

The Course of the Scandinavian Invasions to *c.* 954 A.D.

The Viking Age lasted the best part of three centuries, and it is by no means easy to decide the most convenient and useful point to break a narrative account of the impact of the Northerners. Their aims, methods, and achievements varied from generation to generation and right to the end provide the historian with a complicated pattern of human nature and circumstance. There were settlers in the 8th century; there were raiders and pillagers in the eleventh. Active Danish, Norwegian and Swedish traders performed their more peaceful function throughout. Nevertheless if a break has to be made 954 represents as convenient a dividing point as any, marking as it does the end of the attempt to keep the north of England in a Scandinavian/Irish political orbit.

Within the first of these periods, *c.* 786–954, each of the main communities suffered in different ways and at slightly different periods, interlocked and interdependent, and connected also with the ebb and flow of Viking invasion on the Continent, especially in Normandy. It would be wrong therefore to attempt a further division into sub-periods, and an attempt is made in the following pages to highlight the main events as they occur in the separate communities, always bearing in mind the repercussions of these events on the other parts of the British Isles. Scotland has been treated first because of a natural priority in time and also because of peculiarities in its development which make it essential to grasp the situation in the North if invasion elsewhere is to be understood. Ireland is treated next for a similar chronological reason, and Wales is brought into the story to round off the picture of events on the western seaboard of Britain. Last of all in place but not importance is England. Rather more than half this chapter will be taken up with English affairs not only because events are so much more fully recorded in relation to them, but also because truly decisive happenings not only for the British but for European history took place on English soil during these years.

Scotland

Yet we start with something of a paradox. The historian has narrative evidence for raids on England late in the 8th century. His record of Scottish affairs is meagre in the extreme. How then can we assert with such sureness that priority shall be given to Scottish affairs? The answer is to be found in the work of the archaeologist and in that of the place-name expert. It is from their findings that the material comes to enable us to argue in favour of a settlement in the North in the course of the late 8th and early 9th centuries.

Scandinavian activity concerned itself with three principal geographical areas: the Northern Isles, the Caledonian mainland, and the Western Isles extending as far as the Isle of Man. Most interesting and clearcut are the Northern Isles of Orkney and Shetland. These consist of two virtual archipelagos of islands, nearly 70 in the Orkneys and about 100 in the Shetlands, only comparatively few of which are now inhabited. In historic times they were very much the province of the wind and the waves. Communications were of necessity by sea, and skilled seamen were needed to man the boats in what are often tempestuous and dangerous waters. Yet at several points in time these islands have been at the centre of important movements of people and of civilisation. Megalithic monuments such as the stone-built tombs of Maeshowe in Orkney, great henge monuments such as the Ring of Brodgar or the Ring of Bookan, the well-excavated and much discussed village site of Skara Brae, all testify to the vitality of the inhabitants of the island in the two millennia B.C. At a later stage the fantastic brochs, the stone-built tower of which at the best-known broch site at Clickhimin near Lerwick still stands 17 feet high, speak of a strong organised military community spreading from the mainland throughout the islands in the 2nd and 3rd centuries A.D. Modern man is rightly amazed at the skill of the sailors of these periods from the Neolithic to the Early Iron Age, braving successfully the northern waters in their frail craft. But though it is wrong to think of the islands as perpetually on the fringe of civilisation, it is probably true to say that never were they as much at the centre of a great movement as during the Viking Age.

Great mysteries surround the arrival of the Scandinavians in Orkney and Shetland. Both the state and nature of the original

45

inhabitants and the date of the Scandinavian descent have been matter for dispute, and only very slowly are acceptable conclusions based on acceptable evidence being presented. These mysteries were as great to historians in the Middle Ages as they are to historians in the twentieth century. The early thirteenth-century historians of the history of Norway took refuge in a set of good stories:

Concerning the Orkney Islands

Picts (*Peti*) and Gaelic priests (*Papae*) were the first inhabitants of these islands. The Picts were scarcely more than pygmies in stature, toiling wonderfully mornings and evenings at building their towns, but at midday losing all their strength and, out of sheer terror hiding themselves in subterranean dwellings. The islands were called not Orkneys but the land of the Picts, wherefore to this day the sea which separates the islands from Scotland is called the Pentland Firth (*Petlandicum mare*). . . . We know practically nothing about the people who were then the inhabitants. The priests were called *papae* because of the white robes they wore, for in the Germanic tongue all priests (*clerici*) are called *papae*. There is to this day an island which they call Papey. . . . In the days of Harold Fairhair . . . pirates of the kin of the most powerful prince Ragnall, crossing the North Sea with a great fleet, destroyed them and deprived them of their accustomed habitation and subjected the islands to their own power. Whence, protected more securely in their winter quarters they made their forays in summer, exercising tyrannical rule now among the English, now the Scots and now the Irish, to the point where they subjugated to their authority Northumbria in England, Caithness in Scotland, and Dublin and other seaports in Ireland.[1]

This account and saga accounts which also emphasised settlement in the later 9th century in the reign of Harold Fairhair were somewhat hard to reconcile with archaeological evidence which pointed to Scandinavian presence in the islands at least as early as *c.* 800 A.D. Norwegian historians emphasising the peaceful nature of the Norse penetration were also a little affronted by the suggestion of massacre and virtual extermination of the original inhabitants. A. W. Brögger was so confounded by the difficulties that he suggested settlement in a land that was virtually empty, 'a veritable museum' of deserted brochs, farms and outbuildings.[2] Pictish names and other traces of native presence could be explained on analogy with Iceland, by the importation of thralls to serve the new Norse masters. Modern scholars would rather hold that the Picts were overwhelmed politically, linguistically, culturally and socially but not necessarily exterminated. Similarities in style of house-building and of simple grave construction have been held to suggest some cultural transmission from Picts to Norseman. Particularly compelling are the modern excavations by Dr Anna Ritchie at Buckquoy on the northwest coast of Orkney which have shown on one site a full continuity in domestic architecture. Recent quite brilliant work on the Pictish languages confirms that a Pictish group inhabited the islands. Placename evidence points to the presence of some Goidelic Scots. The islands can indeed now be taken to have been inhabited and Christianised when the Scandinavians arrived towards the end of the 8th century with the political evidence slightly in favour of a decade or so before 800 A.D. rather than after it. The evidence for serious raids from the north both down the east and west coasts of Britain in the years 786–820 makes it exceedingly unlikely that the Northern Isles were not well known to the raiders. Finds made at the most important of the excavations yet undertaken at Jarlshof in Shetland, suggest that the peaceful farming community there indulged in occasional raids and forays against the Celtic West.[3]

The initial settlement must have been made with some force and determination, enough to ensure that the indigenous Christian inhabitants were completely conquered. Assuming that this took place about 800 the most acceptable chronological pattern for later developments would be that of steady recruitment throughout the raiding period, say to about 865 or 870, with a renewed and intensified colonisation period following the political upheavals attendant upon Harold Fairhair's consolidation of the Norwegian kingdom in the last decades of the 9th century. During this long period the original inhabitants either found themselves squeezed out of all economic activity which would permit them to maintain an independent organised social life of their own, or driven to seek refuge with their farming on the mainland. The parallel with the Anglo-Saxon invasions of south and east Britain in the 5th and 6th centuries is striking, though there are also marked contrasts. Evidence of cultural revival is rather stronger in the north, with Pictish motifs reappearing as late as the early tenth century. There is also some evidence for religious revival, though not all scholars would agree on the strength of this evidence, and the saga accounts of the conversion of the Orkneys by Olaf Tryggvasson would certainly suggest a predominantly heathen community in the north as late as the early eleventh century.

On one fact all authorities are agreed. The settlement of the Northern Isles was a true settlement, and came principally from Norway. Very delicate and subtle linguistic work has further suggested an overwhelming preponderance of settlers from the western fjords, especially though not exclusively from Rogadal and the *fylkir* to the south of Bergen.

The best evidence for the type of settlement effected in the Northern Isles comes from the remarkable site of excavation at Jarlshof. This site at Sumbergh Head, the southernmost point of the Shetlands, attracted human settlers from Neolithic times through the Bronze Age to the time of the broch-builders and the Viking Age. The first Scandinavian settlement has been dated to the first half of the 9th century and consisted of a characteristic small farming community. A rectangular house *c.* 70 foot by 20 foot was the chief building, a longhouse with the longer walls curved in slightly at the ends in a way reminiscent of houses roofed by upturned boats. Beside the house itself there were outbuildings identified as a byre, a smithy and a bath-house. Animal bones and midden deposits suggest that farming activities predominated in this community – even fishing playing a relatively minor role. The presence of many stone loom-weights indicates the importance of textile activity. Bone combs, exquisitely carved pins with animal, axe-head and thistle decoration, speak of considerable artistic development. The peaceful nature of the settlemement can probably be exaggerated. Virtual absence of weapons does not necessarily imply peace: rather it shows that the settlers took good care of their weapons and did not lose them. Later saga accounts refer to the settlers as ness-takers; men who, secure at sea, threw up hasty fortifications across the neck of a headland or peninsula to give themselves a base on land. Peaceful farming could come later when the settlement and land-taking are complete.[4]

We know something of their institutions from Scandinavian analogies in the homeland and to some extent from archaeological and place-name evidence. The *bondir*, a peasant-farmer, represented the basic unit in society, head of a household with odal rights. Military leadership was supplied by sea-captains, but there is no evidence of an aristocratic principle at work, and no evidence for the transportation of rank over the North Sea except for the special respect shown to some men who may have been capable of boasting of royal blood in their veins. In the first place of settlement there was little room for the flourishing of lordly principles. We hear of men who styled themselves *jarl* but of no jarl (or earl) of Orkney or Shetland until the close of the 9th or beginning of the tenth century.

From their headquarters in the north, Scandinavians spread south to the mainland and west to the Western Isles in the course of the 9th and early tenth centuries. It is hard to establish a chrono-

1. Early historic Scotland, from A. A. M. Duncan *Scotland, the Making of the Kingdom.*

logical sequence because only at Jarlshof and less so at Underhoull in Shetland and at Birsay in Orkney is there any clear indication of how these settlements thrived during these centuries. Political history helps a little, though it must be recognised that the picture given in the saga of the deeds of the earls of Orkney are themselves distorted by the needs of the narrator. The first prominent ruler was Sigurd, brother of Ragnall Møre (and so probably the uncle of Rollo, first duke of Normandy) at the end of the 9th century. From the Orkney centre he exercised some authority over Shetland and also over Caithness. Place-names suggest Scandinavian penetration further south in Ross and Cromarty and Sutherland at the expense of Pictish power. The distribution of early Scandinavian names suggests that their movement was seaborne, that they established their little farming Jarlshof-type centres along the river valleys, relying on the rough pasture of the highland shielings to supplement and support the exiguous products of the poor barley-growing lands of the scanty lowlands. Whether they displaced or intermarried with the native population is uncertain, probably more of the latter than the former. The limit of Scandinavian penetration was indeterminate, far-reaching and longlasting in the modern shires as far south as the great spread of Inverness-shire, north of the great firth, no more than scattered, spasmodic, and temporary on the eastern seaboard of the Moray Firth and Aberdeenshire. The widest extent was probably reached as late as the middle of the eleventh century under the jarldom of Thorfinn the Mighty (d. 1065).

Expansion along the western coast of Scotland is more intelligible yet not easy to reconstruct in detail. The magnet was undoubtedly Ireland, but the trail of iron filings left scattered down to the Irish Sea, the Hebrides, Outer and Inner and the islands as far south as Man, must not be regarded as mere accidents of fate, refuges for those who had failed to reach their haven in Ireland. The islands had positive attractions for Scandinavian farmers and fishermen seeking a home and land for permanent settlement. Linguistic evidence, as we shall see later, suggests a degree of peaceful intermingling of Celtic and Scandinavian stocks. Archaeological evidence is scanty but sufficient to suggest an early accord between pagan newcomers and Christian inhabitants, and an early conversion to Christianity. In some places there was full continuity in the use of land. Christian cemeteries were used for pagan burials. Sculptural evidence is particularly strong in the Isle of Man to indicate that Celtic and Viking populations lived together in amity. A surprising number of Celtic names appear carved in Scandinavian runes. In an age when communications depended on the sea the islands continued to be treated as a unit, with two obvious geographical sub-units – the Nordreys and Sudreys. The notion of political allegiance to Norway continued to persist practically and actively in the north, to 1468–9, and strongly in the south to the middle of the thirteenth century.

Ireland

The pattern of Viking onslaught on Ireland is clear, though the detail surrounding events, personalities, and even the certain identification of personalities, is often obscure. Early raids between 795 and the 830s were followed by a period of intense settlement in fortified townships on the sea-coast. The key figures in the political events of this phase were the militant pagan Norwegian Thorgils (or Turgeis), a Norwegian chieftain of royal stock, Olaf of Dublin, and – far and away the most important of the three – Ivar the Boneless, a Dane and the son of the Viking chieftain, Ragnar Lothbrok, whose death in Northumbria is said to have triggered off the main Viking attack on England in 865. During these middle years of the 9th century a Scandinavian presence in the harbours and ports of Ireland, especially in Dublin, was firmly established. A change comes over the pattern with the Scandinavian successes in England in the late 860s. From that time forward for the best part of a century the history of the Vikings in Ireland was inextricably mixed up with Viking enterprise in England, intimately and directly with enterprise in northern England. Larger Viking ambitions ended in failure. The sons of Ivar and his grandsons were constantly active and often formidable, but they failed to establish a permanent dynasty.[5] Dublin and York, the two twin power centres of their family – and of other Viking families too – were sometimes for brief periods brought under the rule of one man but more often went their own paths. The Irish Sea which the Vikings dominated for decades proved inadequate as a reservoir of political strength. The return of Olaf Cuaran, son of Sihtric, from York to Dublin in 952, followed by the eclipse of the Scandinavian kingdom of York itself in 954 put an end to the most extravagant of Scandinavian aims in Britain.

Wider Viking ambitions, conspicuously expressed in attempts to create a living kingdom of York and Dublin but not confined to English ventures, had an important bearing on native Irish history. The Scandinavian impact was tremendous but the danger of the complete Scandinavianisation of Ireland was lessened considerably by these wider preoccupations. In the event the first long phase of Scandinavian attack left the mainland of Ireland overwhelmingly in Irish hands. The dominant note in Viking settlement was more attuned to the sea than to the land, the typical creation the fortified port not the cluster of farms of the Scottish Islands. More often than not within Ireland itself the Vikings appeared as yet another element in the inter-tribal warfare of Ireland, now allying with the men of the North, now with the Southerners, now fighting in unison, now among themselves, Dane against Norwegian or Norwegian against Norwegian.

Detailed record of political events is spasmodic and at times ambiguous. The 790s, which had seen the sack of Lindisfarne, also saw Viking disaster strike the monks of Iona and the monks settled on the island of Lambey north of Dublin off the Leinster coast. In 795 Northmen sailing south from Skye, possibly the same group that had found Iona a profitable target, plundered and burnt the church at Lambey in the first recorded attack on Irish soil. For close on 40 years sporadic raids on ill-defended monasteries continued to harass the Irish, though as recent scholars have been quick to point out not all the raiding and destruction should be attributed to Northern sources. These early Viking attacks seems to have coincided with a loss of moral force among the Christian Irish themselves. Churches and monasteries which for centuries had been regarded as sacrosanct became the prey of Irish ravagers as well as of Norse. At some time in the 830s raiding gave way to permanent settlement associated with the shadowy and heroic figure of the pagan Norwegian prince Thorgils, or *Turgeis*. He seems to have made the North his political centre after the capture of Armagh, but under his tutelage if not always under his direct protection Norwegians set up their coastal strongholds at Anagassan on the coast of Louth, Waterford, Wexford, and most important of all at Dublin. The open Atlantic held no terrors for the Norwegians. They set up a small settlement on the Shannon at Limerick and, almost incredibly, at a later date even attacked the savage, isolated and one would imagine virtually impregnable, rock islet monastery of Skellig Michael, eight miles from the coast of Kerry, towering, almost sheer, cliff high above the turbulent and treacherous Atlantic. Thorgils, an intense pagan, roused Christian feeling against him, and was captured and drowned by his enemies in 845. Olaf of Dublin and Ivar the Boneless and his successors sustained and strengthened what were virtually pirate bases, particularly Dublin with its fine commanding position on the Irish Sea. There was no serious attempt whatsoever to conquer Ireland. In this phase of Viking impact on Ireland right the way through to Olaf Cuaran's failure at York in 951, Scandinavian ambitions, Norwegian and Danish, were concentrated on the ports which they themselves constructed and fortified. They provided a constant irritant to the Irish political body, dabbling in tribal politics, creating a new Irish/Scandinavian society only in their fortified townships on the coast, acting at times openly as mercenaries. Under provocation Cearbhall, the native king of Leinster, sacked Dublin in 902 and it took the concerted efforts of a new Scandinavian attack under Ragnall (Rægnvold), the grandson of Ivar, in the second decade of the tenth century, to re-establish the Viking coastal hold from Waterford to Dublin. Ireland was treated as something of a milch-cow, a source of supply of slaves for use in colonising schemes elsewhere, notably in Iceland, and as the essential base and haven for attacks on England and Wales. One of the reasons why the story of Scandinavian attacks on Britain appears at times in the records to have been so scrappy and uncoordinated is because so little is said of the steady recouping, refurbishing, and re-equipping that was the special function of the Irish strongholds, notably Dublin, in this massive enterprise. It is probable that as many Viking attacks were launched east from Dublin as south from Orkney, and virtually certain that more came immediately east from the Irish ports than direct from Norway.

Wales

The Welsh by reason of geography, favourable political accident, and possibly because of their relative poverty, weathered the Viking attacks in the period *c.* 790–950 with surprising success. Danish attacks in the 790s were repulsed with heavy loss and later attacks in the 850s and 860s appear to have been little more than probing raids on the lowlands of Gower and Anglesey, part and parcel of the general unrest which was to culminate in the main onslaught against England in 865. Wales does not provide a good coastline for hostile forces to attack. The fine sandy beaches of Anglesey, Pembrokeshire and Gower, are more than countered by difficulties of approach, treacherous currents, and uncertain winds.

The indirect effect of Scandinavian pressure was undoubtedly great. In the 9th century Rhodri Mawr, prince of Gwynedd, 844–78, maintained the integrity of his principality in spite of serious attempts to set up Scandinavian settlements in Anglesey. He defeated and killed the Danish leader Gorm in what seems to have been a campaign of more than usual importance in 855. Even so, for a short while in the last years of his reign he was forced, after defeats at the hands of the Danes, to seek exile in Ireland. Anglesey was again attacked in the early tenth century, first by Vikings suffering from Irish victories at Dublin in 902 and later in consequence of the general surge of Viking activity in the Irish Sea area after 914. Neither attack was completely successful, the first diverted to Chester and so opening up an important stage in the settlement of north-west England, the second no more than a giant raid, a by-product of Viking restoration of their hold on Irish ports. South Wales was subject to greater strains. Pembrokeshire, offering a long and easy line of entry through Milford Haven, suffered sporadic attack and possible limited settlement along the Haven. The recoil of the remnants of the great hordes which failed to crush Alfred's Wessex led to severe raiding to the north as well as to the south of the Severn Sea. In 914, as a by-product of intensified Viking activity, and possibly in direct consequence of the settlement of Normandy, a Viking host from Brittany, led by the two earls, Ohter and Hroald, ravaged the Welsh coast and penetrated the Wye Valley as far as Archenfield where they captured Bishop Cyfeiliog, bishop of Llandaff. The bishop was in fact ransomed for £40 by the English king. Native developments in the south as well as the north helped to safeguard Wales. One of the greatest of medieval Welsh rulers, Hywel Dda, Hywel the Good, flourished during the first half of the tenth century. He was a close friend of the West Saxon dynasty, worked well in harmony with them, and cooperated fully in meeting the Scandinavian menace which afflicted Christian Wales and England alike. About 920 he consolidated his hold on south-west Wales by campaigns in Pembrokeshire which may have had the effect of limiting Viking activity in that sensitive area. By 942 he was virtually master of all Wales. From the first long drawn-out phase of Scandinavian attack Wales appeared to have emerged without mortal wound and indeed strengthened. Hywel had protected the Welsh people and offered prospect of a greater unity very much as Alfred and his successors had offered protection and prospects to the West Saxon and the English.

England

English affairs are better recorded than affairs in the Celtic world with the result that we can follow at times in great detail the ebb and flow of Scandinavian attack on England. The overall pattern is quite clear. Raids in the later part of the 8th century were followed by a period of calm, broken in the 830s by more serious attempts at colonisation. The correspondence with events in Ireland is striking, but the English were wealthier, stronger, and better equipped to stand the initial strain. Their resistance was successful and the Danes did not winter in England until the year 850–1. From that point onwards however the momentum of attack grew, and serious colonisation started, with a climax reached about the year 878 when Alfred, king of Wessex, succeeded in checking the Danish advance. During the last decades of the century an uneasy political truce was established, leaving the Danes in command of most of England to the east and north of Watling Street and the river Lea, and the house of Wessex in substantial command of unconquered Christian England. Norwegian/Irish penetration of the north-west intensified in the early part of the tenth century but an attempt to set up a straggling trading-based kingdom of Dublin and York failed. Under the leadership of a series of capable kings, greater Wessex re-absorbed the Danish-held territories so that by 954 the political shape of a unified Christian or Christianised England was fully formed.

In a famous entry (for 789) the Anglo-Saxon Chronicle records the first coming of the Vikings to England during the reign of King Brihtric (786–802). Three boatloads of Norwegians from Hörthaland arrived off the Dorset coast. A king's reeve, apparently under the impression that they were traders, tried to force them to come to the king's residence. He himself had been stationed at Dorchester. The Norsemen turned on him and killed the reeve and his men. Four years later the Chronicle records the fearsome sack of the monastery at Lindisfarne and we are given the well-attested date of 8 June 793 for this event. Further ravaging (not without loss) is reported from Northumbria in 794 at the monastery of *Donemuthan*, presumably Jarrow/Wearmouth. A feature of these entries, reinforced by the voluminous correspondence which passed between England and the Frankish court of Charles the Great on the subject of the sack of Lindisfarne, is the completely unexpected nature of these happenings. The reeve at Dorchester had expected to find peaceful traders on the Dorset coat, men from within the civilised world, who would subscribe to the customs and conventions of the community and who would go peacefully with their goods to the royal residence. Alcuin writing from Charles's court to the Northumbrian king gives the best insight into the shock and horror with which the sack of Lindisfarne was greeted throughout the Christian world.

Lo, it is nearly 350 years that we and our fathers have inhabited this most lovely land, and never before has such terror appeared in Britain as we have now suffered from a pagan race, nor was it thought that such an inroad from the sea could be made. Behold the church of St Cuthbert spattered with the blood of the priests of God, despoiled of all its ornaments; a place more venerable than all in Britain is given as a prey to pagan peoples.[6]

55

It was natural for Alcuin to look for an inner explanation of these happenings, to attribute them to sin, to fornication, avarice, robberies, even to the dress, the way of wearing the hair, the luxurious habits of the princes and people. The good Northumbrians are exhorted to look to their trimming of beard and hair, in which they have wished to ape the pagan. And the lesson is made plain when Alcuin writes:

> What should be expected for other places, when the divine judgment has not spared this holy place?

These early raids were Norwegian and were accompanied by, and possibly a product of, sporadic settlement in the islands to the north and west of Britain. The Danes were also active, stirred up, as some observers thought, by the ferment which resulted from the creation of the great Frankish Empire by Charles the Great. Reduction of the independence of continental Saxony and Frisia contributed to native Danish unrest. But for the first 30 years or so of the 9th century most Danish turbulence seemed to be directed against fellow Danes. Not until the 830s was a substantial proportion of Danish energy unleashed against the Western world. England now became a prime target for their unwelcome attentions.

The Anglo-Saxon Chronicle, which was put together in the form we know it in the 890s, becomes our chief source of information concerning the Scandinavian attacks.[7] Supplemented at times by entries in continental chronicles it provides a picture of constant attack or threat of attack throughout the 9th century. In 835 a heavy raid was directed against the Isle of Sheppey. The east and south-east continued during this phase of onslaught to bear the brunt of piratical raids. The pirates went where the wealth was greatest. Twice, in 850 in the Isle of Thanet, and in 854 in Sheppey, there is record of Danish armies wintering in England. Throughout the whole 30 years to 865 there is however, no clear-cut attempt at permanent colonisation. The generation was concerned with loot and sporadic raids rather than systematic probing of defences with a view to stable settlement.

Danish ambitions during the last third of the 9th century were of a very different nature. The moment of change came in autumn 865. An army, described by the Chronicle as large, landed in East Anglia. Its leadership was principally in the hands of the sons of Ragnar Lothbrok, or Leather-Breeches, especially Ivar the Boneless and Healfden and Ubba. It would be wrong, however, to suggest unified command. There were many kings and earls with the Danish host. It is highly probable that the most meaningful element in the leadership was the personal authority of the sea-captains who commanded the individual longships and the warriors who sailed in them. A captain of royal blood would be known as a king and might exert loose authority over a small fleet; a powerful captain, again possibly exercising authority over a small fleet, might from past rank and present power be known as earl (*jarl*). They operated as armies in face of strong native reaction. The ferocity of their attacks is proven by all manner of evidence: for example exact work on the deposit of coin hoards in England has proved beyond doubt that a substantial peak occurred in the deposit of hoards during the decade 865–75. Their army organisation persisted to some measure as conquest gave place to settlement. But always underneath the façade of regional unity existed the independence of the smaller group, the ships' crews that continued to give protection as further immigrants settled and intensified the Danish hold on a large section of northern and eastern England.

The political story of the succeeding years is intimately bound up with the career of King Alfred of Wessex, the one Christian leader with the strength and will to check the Danish hosts. From 865 to 871, the year of battles in the course of which Alfred succeeded to the West Saxon throne, Danish victories were continuous. They used East Anglia as their base for supply and recruitment from the autumn of 865 to the autumn of 866. Extensive damage to Thetford, and some evidence for incendiarism in the cathedral of North Elmham may have occurred at this stage. The Danes were especially anxious to equip themselves with horses and it was as a mounted host that they embarked on the conquest of Northumbria in 866–7, in the course of which the great monastery at Whitby was sacked. York itself was captured on 21 March. Northumbria had been weakened by a civil war in which King Osbert had been rejected by his people who had chosen Aella, a man not of the royal stock, and the reputed slayer of Ragnar, as their king. The Vikings found such a situation to their taste, wintered at York, and after Osbert and Aella in a temporary reluctant reconciliation were both killed in a partially successful attack on the city, the Vikings appear to have set up an English prince who exercised nominal rule there *sub potestate Danorum*. The Danes then wintered at Nottingham, after ravaging Mercia and forcing the Mercian king Burgred to buy peace from them. In the autumn of 868 they descended again on York and the following year they moved back into East Anglia, defeating and killing the East Anglian king Edmund (855–69), who was quickly honoured as a saint and martyr by his countrymen. His death, probably as a captive in Danish hands, on 20 November 869, is immensely important. It marks the end of native Christian kingship in East Anglia. The impact on the Scandinavians themselves was also to prove formidable; in the twelfth century the conversion of Iceland was dated 1000 years after the birth of our Lord and 130 after the death of King Edmund. Northumbria also fell completely under Danish control though for the time being Egbert, a puppet Englishman, bore the royal title. The time was now ripe for a trial of strength with the strongest surviving English kingdom, the kingdom of Wessex.

From the autumn of 870 to King Alfred's death in 899, the dominant political theme was indeed the struggle between the West Saxons and the Danes. When the campaign opened Alfred was not yet king. He was the *secundarius*, the young heir-apparent to his brother King Ethelred, 22 or 23 years of age. The Danes moved their army headquarters to Reading and for a solid twelvemonth strove to break West Saxon resistance. This year of battles saw victories on both sides. Danish checks at Englefield and Ashdown (where one Danish king and five earls were killed) were followed by English reverses at Basing and *Meretun*. King Ethelred died in April 871 and Alfred succeeded. English defeats at Reading and Wilton forced the new king to buy peace from the Danes who were now in secure control of the Thames estuary and of London. But Alfred had at the least preserved his own authority over the West Saxons.

Alfred's reign may be divided conveniently into three clearly defined political and military phases. For the first seven years the Danes held the full initiative and it was much in the balance whether or not the whole of England would fall into their grasp. The middle years of the reign, from 878 to 891, were a period of consolidation and of the marking out of new though in the event impermanent political frontiers. During the last eight years from 891 to 899, the last serious threat came of a political conquest of Wessex, a threat which came to an end with the break up of the 'great horde', the *micel here* as the Chronicle called it, in the summer of 896. It is customary to read this epic story from the defenders' point of view. Undoubtedly Alfred was a great king and his achievements played a dominant part in the shaping of a united Christian monarchy in England. He preserved Christian Wessex as a nucleus of a united England. He heightened the idea of a Christian monarchy by precept and example. It is salutary on occasions, however, to look at the political situation from the other point of view. Concentration on English resilience and awareness of ultimate English political success should not lead to neglect of Danish achievement and permanent social success. From 871 to 878 the Danish armies extended their hold intensively over East Anglia, Northumbria and the greater part of Mercia. They inflicted a decisive defeat on the Mercian king Burgred in 874. They initiated, under the leadership of Healfden, an agrarian settlement in Northumbria in 876. They effected a rough partition of Mercia in 877. The following year, 878, was the year of decision. The Danes under the command of Guthrum overran the greater part of Wessex, forced Alfred to take refuge in the marshes of Athelney, and came within an ace of achieving complete conquest. King Alfred's emergence from Athelney and his rallying of his warrior-thegns brought this phase of Danish onslaught to its conclusion. The Treaty of Wedmore between Alfred and Guthrum was followed by the conversion of Guthrum to Christianity. From the Christian West Saxon point of view Edington and Wedmore have intelligibly been interpreted as a saving mercy. This is not the only possible point of view. The terms of Wedmore did nothing to loosen the hold of the Danish armies on territories they had already occupied. Indeed Guthrum's army remained quartered in Chippenham throughout the summer of 878. Only in the autumn did they withdraw to Cirencester in English Mercia and not until 879 did they withdraw east to embark on a systematic settlement of East Anglia. The Danes could pride themselves on having won recognition now within the Christian community itself. The settlement in some ways represented a legitimisation of their authority, though the situation was probably not completely clarified until 885–86. The boundary between Danish dominated England and English England lay through the old kingdom of Mercia in a line running roughly from north-west to south-east, from Chester along Watling Street to the river Lea and so to London. This boundary between what was later known as the Danelaw and English England became a permanent feature of the social and institutional life of these islands. London remained, temporarily it is true, in Danish hands. The campaigning season of 878 had resulted in a military defeat at Edington, but the Danish army remained essentially intact and formidable. Its leader, Guthrum, was strengthened rather than weakened by his baptism. The attempted conquest of Wessex had failed, but attractive possibilities were now open in the east free from fear of West Saxon interference, and to some measure in accord with West Saxon wishes. The Chronicle records carefully that in 879 Guthrum, now a Christian king who took on the baptismal name of Athelstan, shared out the land in East Anglia. The kingdom of St Edmund had passed into Danish but not into heathen hands. It is possible, given their likely limitation in manpower and their assumed ambitions to win land for farming, that the Treaty of Wedmore gave the Danes of this first invasion precisely what they themselves wanted, an opportunity to regularise their own territorial settlement in the North and East.

The middle years of Alfred's reign following the Treaty of Wedmore to the arrival of the great host from the Continent in 891 represent a working out of the consequences of the political movements of the '70s. Guthrum died in 890 and on the whole upheld the promises to keep the peace which he had sworn to his godfather, King Alfred, during the baptismal ceremonies of 878. Alfred made one formidable advance in 886 when he occupied London. This was part of a move to free the Thames estuary from further piracy and was further associated with internal English political happenings. We are told by the Chronicle in connection with the move on London that the English people who were not under subjection to the Danes submitted to him, and further that he entrusted the borough to the control of the *ealdorman* Ethelred. Alfred was now the sole surviving ruling prince of the old royal stocks and it was natural that the surviving English authorities should look to him. The ealdorman Ethelred, was a Mercian who quickly became if he was not so already – the date of the marriage is uncertain – Alfred's own son-in-law. He and his wife Aethelflæd, later known as the Lady of the Mercians, are crucial figures in the successful attempt to bring the West Saxons and the English Mercians into peaceful union. The issue of what was to be the most attractive type of silver penny of Alfred's later reign, a coin with the London monogram inscribed on the reverse, undoubtedly dates from 886.[8] The principal Danish endeavours in fact seem during the '80s to have been directed towards continental Europe. One of the great difficulties of dealing with a period as fluid politically as the 9th century consists precisely in the complicated interaction of movements of these very mobile Scandinavians on the various more settled communities of the West. Within the area that we can now conveniently call the Danelaw consolidation of agrarian settlement and retention of military organisation are both apparent. Land settlement and the introduction of immigrants were achieved under the discipline of armies which maintained fortified headquarters at Northampton, Cambridge, Tempsford, Thetford and Huntingdon. The 'five boroughs' of the north-east Midlands, Leicester, Nottingham, Derby, Lincoln and Stamford, were probably fortified effectively at this time. In the north York dominated the whole area, rapidly developing into a powerful Scandinavian fortified market, comparable with Dublin in its commercial aspects and more important than Dublin in that York also emerged as the political heart of a vigorous colonising movement in Northumbria. Evidence from the later histories of the see of St Cuthbert at Durham, coupled with possible interpretation of the coin evidence, suggests a succession of kings at York prepared to work with the archbishops (Archbishop Wulfhere who was prominent in the savage early crises of the 870s was still active in the early 890s). Guthfrith, who may well have become the outstanding Viking leader in 880 after Healfden's death, enjoyed a good reputation among Christian historians, possibly because of the part he played in the transfer of the see at Lindisfarne to Chester-le-Street, and was buried in August 895 at his head church, presumably the cathedral at York. Excavations at York, though unspectacular, have been enough to suggest a strong trading community at a very early stage. By 891 a whole mass of Scandinavian and Anglo-Scandinavian communities were established in the Danelaw. Some of the Vikings had been settled in their own farms or urban dwellings at York for half a generation and more. Some retained their native paganism but others had followed the example of Guthrum and Guthfrith and had accepted Christianity. Stone carving and sculpture for example in the Vale of Pickering, especially at Middleton, indicates a coming together of Christian and pagan motifs at a very early stage in the settlement of Yorkshire, probably from this very generation. For a people with no native coinage the Scandinavians took early to the use of coins. Already by the last decade of the late 9th century coins were struck in Danish-occupied England, some by English moneyers recruited specially to York and to East Anglia where religious motifs and inscriptions on the coins indicate the intensity of religious beliefs in new converts. Not all can have welcomed the new irruption of Scandinavian despoilers which came to afflict England in the 890s.[9]

The troubles of the 890s were a direct consequence of the stiffening of continental resistance to Danish attack. The successful defence of Paris 886–7 was followed by Arnulf's victory at the battle of the river Dyle (near Louvain) in 891. At some time between September 891 and September 892 a force of 250 ships sailed from Boulogne, carrying their horses with them, landing at the estuary of the river Lympne in south-east Kent. Alfred's defensive measures were still incomplete and the half-built, poorly defended fortress at or near Appledore was swiftly overrun. Danish reinforcements under Haesten set up a further camp at Milton in north-east Kent. The details of the campaigns of the following three years were carefully preserved by a contemporary witness. The strategic heart of the matter is clear enough. Formidable Danish armies from their sea-protected fortified bases in Kent and Essex, north and south of the

Thames estuary, with intermittent help from the already settled Danes in East Anglia and Northumbria, attempted to overthrow Alfred's kingdom. They failed. Organisation and systematic defence defeated them. A ring of fortified *burhs* (for the most part well-fortified townships) proved an effective shield for Wessex itself. The loyalty and courage of subordinate *ealdormen*, and of Alfred's son Edward and his son-in-law, Ethelred of Mercia, contributed to Danish defeat. They ravaged deep along the Thames valley, along the Severn valley and into Wales. But in 896 the enterprise was abandoned, the great horde split up, and the Chronicle was able accurately to sum the situation up, recording that 'by the grace of God the army had not on the whole afflicted the English people very greatly'. Alfred's last three years, 896 to his death on 26 October 899, were spent in peace.

The last Danish campaigns which failed are in their way as instructive as the earlier campaigns which succeeded. Women and children were present at the Danish camps in Benfleet. The armies were as ready poised for successful settlement in the 890s as their fathers and kinsfolk had been in the '60s and '70s. They did not succeed in winning a patrimony for themselves in south-east England, let alone Wessex and English Mercia. Not until the successful French campaigns of 911 and 912 20 years later, was territory opened for primarily Danish settlement in what was to become the Duchy of Normandy. Yet a genuine land-hunger existed and a genuine land-hunger was in fact assuaged. The Chronicle tells us that with the disruption of the great army those who had enough property and money bought themselves into the settled communities of Danish East Anglia and Northumbria. No better example could be given both of the success and of the limitations of Alfred's policy. The integrity of English England was preserved. The strength of the settled Scandinavian population, capable of buying and selling land in company with fellow-Scandinavian and English farmers, was increased and intensified in the Danelaw.

The main interest of the second half of the 9th century consists within these islands in the survival of a strong kingdom of Wessex, the nucleus of a kingdom of England, and the provision in the Danelaw of opportunity under temporary Scandinavian military lordship for more concentrated agrarian settlement. This was primarily a Danish venture. Skills learned in the harder but not utterly unsuitable environment of Jutland, Funen and Zealand could be employed to greater advantage in the still underpopulated lands of Lincolnshire, Yorkshire, East Anglia, and the territory of the Five Boroughs. The first half of the tenth century saw the reabsorption of these territories under English lordship. Time was given in the critical 40 years between the Treaty of Wedmore 878 and the decisive campaigns of Alfred's son which reaches a climax in 918 for a whole generation of Danish farmers to be accepted as a permanent and peaceful feature of the landscape of north and east England.

The story of the reconquest of the Danelaw is complicated, partly because it is in the nature of reabsorption. Danish farmers, settled and often Christianised, came to realise that their best hope of peaceful future lay in acceptance of the overlordship of the West Saxon dynasty. A succession of able kings, building further on Alfred's work, showed the right combination of military strength, planning ability, and political sense to bring success to the dynasty. Under Edgar 959–75, a truly united Christian kingdom of England came into being. The progress to such an end was not smooth, nor should it be regarded as inevitable. Vicious cross-currents from Ireland and the Isles – not so much from the Continent, and little direct from Denmark or Norway – tormented the political scene. Under Edward, 899–924, English political authority was reasserted over Eastern Mercia and East Anglia. His son and successor, the brilliant Athelstan, prematurely brought the whole of Northumbria under his control and was widely recognised throughout the British world. The 20 years after his death in 939 was a period of vacillating fortune, complicated by the success of the Norwegian and Irish adventures in Dublin and York. After 954 the situation eased and Edgar's triumphant and peaceful reign may rightly be interpreted as a fitting climax to this hard century of Christian resistance and Danish attack.

From the Scandinavian point of view two features are of outstanding importance. The first of these is the largely unchronicled but firmly evidenced fact of Norwegian-Irish settlement in the north-west of England. The second, a tribute to the success of the Danish farmer rather than the Danish soldier, is the acceptance within the new Christian kingdom of England of a special law, special customs, special agrarian institutions. Both features owed much to tensions within the Scandinavian world itself, to the commercial success which attended the opening up of the regular route from Dublin to York and which should not be masked by the ultimate political failure of the Norwegians at York, and to the fear which developed on the part of the more settled Danish colonists of the earlier generations for the more mobile Norwegian-Irish traders and raiders of the later generations. The settlers accepted Christianity quickly. Two of the outstanding clerics of the first half of the tenth century had powerful contacts with the Danelaw. Theodred,

63

bishop of London, 926–51, effectively looked after much of the East
Anglian kingdom. Oda, archbishop of Canterbury, 941–58, was
himself of Danish birth and said to be a son of a Dane who came to
England with the early settlers. He showed lively interest in the
Fenland country, interceding with the king on behalf of a Cambridgeshire thegn, and receiving land at Ely. His nephew, St Oswald, a son
of Oda's brother, continued the family interest in land and church
affairs in the Danelaw. Heathenism does not appear to have retained
a firm hold on the Scandinavians. Even in the North Riding of
Yorkshire only one certain heathen place-name – Roseberry
Topping – has been identified. Further south an Edgar the Peaceful
was more to the taste of the Danish colonists of the Five Boroughs
than an Eric Bloodaxe.[10]

In the reign of Edward the Elder the first firm steps were taken
towards the reabsorption of the Danes. Permanent fortifications at
strategic points were established throughout western Mercia very
much in line with Alfred's West Saxon defensive policy. A series of
campaigns in 917 and 918 resulted in the seizing of Derby, an
English victory at Tempsford and the rapid reduction or capitulation
of the remaining Danish armies south of the Humber. Moves were
even made by the Scandinavians in York to submit Aethelflæd,
sister of Edward the Elder. Her death on 12 June 918 brought these
moves to a fruitless end. But by the end of the year after the surrender
of Nottingham all the people settled in Mercia, including apparently
the men of Lincoln, submitted to King Edward. The West Saxon
king in 919 spent his best energies ensuring his own peaceful succession
to Mercia and in the meantime Ragnall, the Viking leader from
Dublin, successfully contended for a kingdom in York. The Anglo-
Saxon Chronicle, its natural sympathies heightened by the drama of
events, treats 920 as an *annus mirabilis*, and tells us that in this year
there submitted to King Edward the Scottish king and people,
Ragnall of York, the native ealdorman, Ealdred of Bamborough, with
all the Northumbrians, English, Danish, Northmen, and others – and
the king and people of Strathclyde. Welsh princes are also said to
have submitted to him and to have paid homage to him. Undoubtedly the Chronicler has seized on the poetry of the situation.
Alfred's son was widely recognised as overlord. Modern historians,
while paying tribute to his achievements, have been more sceptical
of the realities of his power. Constant effort was needed to preserve
the union of Mercia and Wessex. In the last year of his reign Edward
had to deal with a rebellion of Mercians in alliance with Welsh
princes focused on Chester. There was nothing he could do north of
the Humber. Danish political independence to the south of that

1. Viking weapons. From the collection at the Norwegian national
museum at Oslo

Left

2. The Gokstad ship. A typical Viking warship, used for a royal burial at the end of the 9th century, excavated from the blue clay that helped to preserve it in 1880, and now on exhibition in the great ship museum in Oslo

Above

3. Stylised head of man from the decoration on the wagon discovered in the Oseberg ship burial, now on exhibition at the Oslo ship museum

4. A reconstruction of the Viking settlement at Jarlshof, Shetland, by Alan Sorrell

5. The Middleton Cross B. One of a group of stone crosses, characteristic of the age of the Viking kingdom of York in East Yorkshire. Depiction of a warrier buried with a spear, knife and axe; the presence of a cockerel may hint at survival of pagan, sacrificial custom

A *Obverse*   A *Reverse*

B *Obverse*   B *Reverse*

Left

6. Trelleborg. An aerial view of one of the great Danish fortresses of the late tenth or early eleventh century, bringing out the strength of the encampments and of the huge boat-shaped houses. Modern investigation stresses the part played by these royal fortresses in maintaining internal order in Denmark

Above

7. Two coins of Sihtric of the Silken Beard, struck by the moneyers Faeremin and Siel at Dublin c. 998–1004. The coins are imitations of Long Cross pennies of Ethelred II

8. Kilpeck. The south porch of this beautiful little Herefordshire church gives plentiful evidence of the survival of Scandinavian artistic elements well into the twelfth century

river had been destroyed. Ragnall, by gaining formal recognition from Edward, had intruded a new potentially dangerous element into English politics.

Meanwhile under cover of all the political battles and the fortifications of Chester, of Thelwall, of Runcorn, of Bakewell, the last of the serious colonisation ventures in England was under way. Place-names are our best guide and inference from cultural development, notably in stone sculpture, also adds to our knowledge. Substantial settlement of an Irish-Norwegian population, men and women from the Scandinavian ports in Ireland, from the Isle of Man, and from the Scottish islands, took place in north-west England. A great hoard of coins deposited at Cuerdale in Lancashire in the earliest years of the century, probably in 903 A.D., gives evidence of the trader-raider moves that went on between Dublin and York side by side with the colonisation. There is a vast quantity of Viking-style sculpture in the north of England, much of it (such as the Dacre and Gosforth crosses) exhibiting clear signs of Hiberno-Norse inspiration, though some shows traits suggesting more direct contact with the Scandinavian homeland. Land not utterly dissimilar to the native Norwegian territory in the Lake District and surrounding territories proved more attractive to men of ultimate Scandinavian descent than to the Anglo-Saxons. In many of the deep valleys of Cumberland and Westmorland the place-name structure suggests that Irish-Scandinavian farmers met a British people with little or no Saxon admixture. The low-lying territories are different; and there in Lancashire and further north around the Solway Firth there is plentiful sign of early Saxon settlement. But over much of Cumberland, Westmorland, north Lancashire and west Yorkshire a vital new element was added to the ethnic pattern in the early decades of the tenth century during the reign of Edward the Elder.

English impotence north of the Humber also threatened at one stage the intrusion and reinforcement of powerful Scandinavian elements in the north-east. A later writer, anxious to establish the history of the see of St Cuthbert, relates how Ragnall (Rægnvold), who later became king of the Vikings at Waterford, won victories north of the Tees, dividing out the conquered territory among his chief soldiers, two of whom are mentioned by name, Scula, who was given an extensive tract roughly 100 square miles or so in extent between the modern Castle Eden and Billingham while Onalafball (who is said to have sworn oaths by Thor and by Odin) received a similar massive grant from Castle Eden to the mouth of the Wear. Sir Frank Stenton, who first noted the true importance of these references as descriptions of precise settlement arrangements, pointed out the similarity in extent of the grants to some of the later sokes of the Danelaw, that is to say, areas over which the landlord exercised special rights of jurisdiction, such as Bolingbroke in Lincolnshire. The arrangement seems to have been reached between 912 and 915, and involved the transmission of clear political and military overlordship. There was not the same intensity of land-taking at this stage by the Irish-Norse elements in the north-east as in the north-west.[11]

Edward's son and successor, Athelstan, 924–39, is remembered as one of the most powerful and spectacular rulers of the dynasty. He had been brought up in Mercia, was readily accepted as king by the Mercians and did more than any other single ruler to bring about by inspiration and deed a true union of West Saxon and Mercian. He strengthened contacts with the Welsh and had little difficulty in expelling the Scandinavians from York in 927. In European affairs he was widely known and respected. Harold Fairhair, king of Norway, treated with him as settled king to settled king, sent a great warship 'with golden prow and purple sail, armed within by a dense row of gilded shields' to Athelstan as a personal present, and permitted his youngest son, Haakon, *Aðalsteins fostri*, to be brought up at Athelstan's court.[12] Although Athelstan's most enduring contribution to the unity of England came in connection with the imposition of effective royal government on southern England he is chiefly remembered for his victory at *Brunanburh* in 937. A full poetic account of the battle was incorporated in the Anglo-Saxon Chronicle. It represented a great victory for the Christian English, led by Athelstan and his young brother Edmund, against a coalition of Scots, British and Scandinavian Irish. The foremost leader and indeed creator of the coalition was Olaf Guthfrithson, the son of the man Athelstan had expelled from York in 927. Olaf survived to take his tattered remnant of an army back to Dublin, but no fewer than five men of royal rank and seven earls were killed from Ireland alone. *Brunanburh* inflicted a sharp check to the political ambitions of the Irish Scandinavian community.[13]

The check proved, however, to be temporary only. With the death of Athelstan in 939 came fresh opportunity. By the end of the year Olaf Guthfrithson was back in York. In 940 he threatened to undo the work of the preceding generation and by a treaty drawn up by the two archbishops of York and Canterbury gained possession of the whole of the Danelaw. His death and the succession of lesser men, his cousin Olaf Sihtricson and his brother Rægnald Guthfrithson in turn destroyed this arrangement. For the last years of Edmund's reign, 944–6, the West Saxon house was again in political control of the North. But a further period of confusion and doubt followed Edmund's assassination in 946. Eric 'Bloodaxe' of Norway, a son of Harold Fairhair, Olaf Sihtricson of Dublin (949–52), and finally for two years Eric again (952–4) ruled at York. The Northumbrians themselves drove him out. His subsequent death at Stainmore brings a symbolic end to this phase of the history of northern England. Eadred, Edmund's successor, played little active part in the final events. Lack of single-minded purpose after the death of Olaf Guthfrithson contributed to the failure of the Irish Scandinavians to set up a permanent political hold on Dublin and York. The intrusion of a formidable and ambitious native Norwegian prince in the person of Eric Bloodaxe underlined the fluidity and complexity of the situation. The hard work inside the southern English kingdoms, the provision of better peace, the identification of christianised Danish farmers with the surviving Christian dynasty helped to ensure that the future hope of a peaceful kingdom rested on the House of Wessex. Yet the time factor alone – the simple chronology of settlement of Dane in east and Norwegian/Irish in north-west – helped to bring it about that the united England of Edgar's reign was a more complex ethnic entity than the familiar Heptarchic pattern of Wessex, Mercia, Northumbria and East Anglia.

4.

Scandinavia during the Later Stages of the Viking Age, *c.* 954–*c.* 1100

It is right and fitting to make a break in the Viking story at the middle of the tenth century. To that point the movement from the North had borne many of the characteristics of the time of folk-wandering. Northmen, from Denmark, Sweden and Norway, sought new homes to settle. The first long phase of Viking movement was a colonising phase. Settlement and consolidation of settlement were the principal features of the later 9th and earlier tenth centuries. The North continued to be active for a further century or more. Some historians looking for a dramatic event to mark the end of the Viking Age have chosen the voyages of Sigurd, Jerusalem-farer, to the Holy Land in the early twelfth century as a symbol of the final acceptance of the Scandinavians into the active heart of Christendom; others have looked further back to the conversion of the Scandinavian homelands in the early eleventh century with the rapid acceptance of Olaf Haroldsson as a saint so soon after his death in battle at Stiklestad in 1030. The strongest case for a single date and a single incident would seem to be for the assassination of St Cnut of Denmark in Roskilde cathedral in 1086. Heavy Viking raids of familiar pattern afflicted the West after the death of St Olaf. St Cnut himself assembled a great fleet at Limfjord for an attempt against England shortly before his death. Yet the raids and troubles and torments inflicted on the West were essentially different from the earlier attack of the 9th and early tenth centuries – and increasingly so as the eleventh century progressed.

Acceptance of Christianity is the essential key to the situation. The distinction between civilised and barbarian rested precisely upon the facts of religious belief during this age. Colonists living in Christian communities accepted the Christian faith as virtually an essential condition of permanence. Viking leaders with ambitions

68

to set up permanent dynasties found it increasingly expedient to profess adherence to Christianity. At home in Scandinavia kings discovered the advantages of a literate universal faith to support them in their tasks of ruling and imposing government among peoples where paganism and localism were ready companions. Conversion lacked the savage rejection of the old religion which accompanied many such movements. Paganism lingered on into the central Middle Ages, tolerated but ineffective in many out-of-the-way parts of the Scandinavian world. But by the third quarter of the eleventh century the Scandinavians were by and large fully accepted as integrated members of Christendom. When Pope Gregory VII (1073–85) imposed his ideas of papal supremacy on the Western world those ideas applied to Nidaros, Roskilde and Lund, to Poland and to Hungary as well as to the traditional Germano-Roman heartlands of the Carolingian Empire. The East and the North had been brought in or had forced themselves in to Western Europe in the course of the Viking centuries.

Denmark was the most important political unit in Scandinavia during this last Viking century, and for the Scandinavian historian it is the consolidation, uneven and precarious at times, of political authority in the hands of a new Danish dynasty that constitutes the chief interest. This is in some ways surprising. For the first 40 years of the tenth century it appeared that the Danes had overreached themselves. Too many of their vigorous young men had gone West over sea. Their colonists had settled successfully large tracts of England and under the leadership of a Norwegian noble house, that of Rollo the son of the earl of Möre, were making an equally successful settlement in the north of France, in the duchy of Normandy. At home, possibly in direct consequence of this drain of manpower, the Danes, as we have seen, met disaster. Their native princes were overthrown and the greater part of Denmark was subject to Swedish rule. In particular the trading centre of Hedeby passed under Swedish control. Complex international events brought about Danish resurgence. After 919 with the election of Henry the Fowler to the German throne, the new Saxon dynasty began to play a dominant part in Western European politics. The culminating point in their dynastic progress came in 962 when Henry's brilliant son, Otto the Great, was crowned emperor at Rome by the Pope, a true successor of Charlemagne; but in the early stages the Saxon rulers, Henry himself, and Otto in the troubled years immediately after his succession in 936, both paid attention to their northern border across the Danish peninsula. Their chief aim was to contain and to Christianise their northern neighbours, and they succeeded in achieving this aim. In 934 Henry the Fowler defeated the Swedes and set up a Danish March. In Denmark itself political power passed away from the wealth of Hedeby to a new dynasty of princes whose base lay at Jelling in south Jutland. The first known rulers of this dynasty, Gorm the Old and his queen, Thyri, are somewhat shadowy figures who flourished about 940. Gorm's son, grandson, and great-grandson, Harold Bluetooth, Sweyn Forkbeard, and Cnut the Great, king of England 1016–35, on the contrary rank among the first in importance of the European rulers of their day.

There is a fine carved stone at Jelling which gives the key to an understanding of Harold Bluetooth's work. It is an artistic creation of great merit with splendid interlacing and carving in which the figure of Christ crucified occupies a dominant position. On it is a runic inscription which reads:

KING HAROLD HAD THIS MONUMENT MADE IN MEMORY OF HIS
FATHER, GORM, AND OF HIS MOTHER THYRI. HAROLD WHO
WON ALL DENMARK AND NORWAY AND MADE THE DANES CHRISTIAN.

The last sentence of the inscription may have been added a shade later than the main text, but the chronological gap cannot have been large and the stone and the carving itself is firmly ascribed to a date between 965 (when Harold became Christian) and 985, the probable date of his death.[1]

Harold's conquest of Norway in the early 960s did not prove complete or permanent, but his own baptism and active fostering of Christianity, together with the associated drawing together of all Denmark into an effective kingdom, were achievements of lasting importance.

Harold's own reign ended in the shadow of personal disaster. His son, Sweyn Forkbeard, turned against him, and the old king after a reign of some 40 years was wounded and died after a short exile in Slav territory. His body was brought back to Denmark and lies buried at Roskilde. Sweyn, his son and successor, governed Denmark effectively for close on 30 years. We shall look later and more closely at the part he was to play in the conquest of England from personal involvement in the giant raids of the early 990s to the final campaign when he resumed personal command in 1013 to his death at Gainsborough on 3 February 1014. The military camps and fortresses discovered by archaeologists and attributed to his reign testify to his military prowess and administrative gifts. These must rank among the most important archaeological contributions to an understanding of the Viking Age. Four such camps are now known and have been investigated: Trelleborg near Slagelse in west

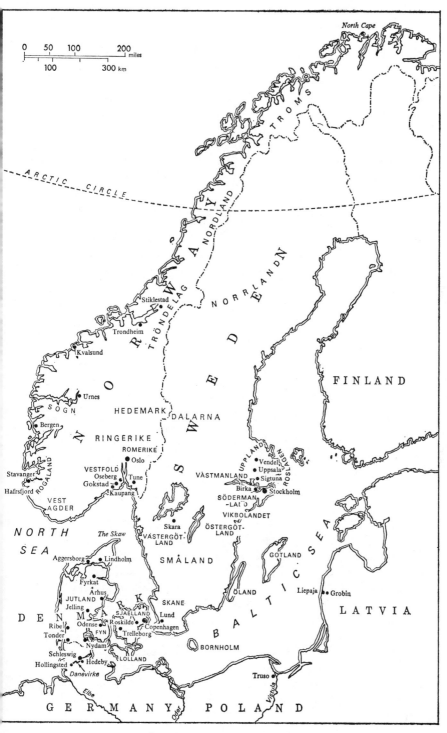

2. Scandinavia in the Viking Age.

Zealand, Aggersborg on the Limfjord in north Jutland, Fyrkat near Hobro in east Jutland, and Nonnebakken at Odense in the island of Funen. They share a common plan, use a common system of mensuration, and were constructed for a common purpose. Aggersborg is the biggest, containing within a circular rampart of 240 metres internal diameter no fewer than 48 identical long wooden houses, each 33 metres in length. At Trelleborg the interior diameter of the rampart is 136 metres and at Fyrkat and Nonnebakken 120 metres. There were 16 identical houses about 30 metres in length at Trelleborg, with a further 15 in the outer defence work, and 16 identical houses (slightly shorter than the main Trelleborg group) at Fyrkat. The Nonnebakken site was built over before exact archaeological investigation was possible. From internal evidence the camps can be dated to *c.* 970–1020, and many scholars (though there is opposition to this view) associate them with plans for Sweyn's massive raids and ultimate conquest of England. It has been estimated that they could have housed 4,000 men if they were indeed primarily 'barracks', but archaeological evidence now suggests that they were fortified settlements of considerable social complexity, including smithies, metal workshops and storehouses. Only the king had the resources to build and preserve such defensive works. The fortresses were well placed to control land communications and played a vital part at a critical time in ensuring the maintenance of royal authority in Denmark even when the king was busy elsewhere overseas in English or Norwegian enterprises.[2]

Sweyn died on English campaign in 1014, but Danish ambitions were brought to fruition by his second son Cnut, finally recognised as sole king in England after the death of Edmund Ironside in November 1016. Denmark itself passed to the eldest son, Harold, who died childless in 1019. Cnut thereupon succeeded also to the Danish throne. Much of the later 1020s were occupied with Norwegian affairs and after the death of the Norwegian prince Olaf Haroldsson (St Olaf) in 1030 Cnut seemed effective master of Denmark, Norway, and England. His international reputation was already high. He had been present as an honoured and exalted guest at the imperial coronation of Conrad II in 1027 and remained on good terms with the Empire. But at this moment in the creation of enduring political units the time was not ripe for the permanent establishment of a North Sea empire. Cnut died still a young man in 1035, and problems of dynastic succession confirmed a natural split along rudimentary national lines. St Olaf, more popular after death than in life with the Norwegians, had left a son, Magnus, who was acclaimed king of Norway in 1035. Cnut's son Harold Harefoot succeeded to England while his other son Harthacnut became king in Denmark. From the tangled fraternal squabbles of 1036–40 Harthacnut emerged Harold Harefoot's successor in England but then lost control in Denmark to the Norwegian powers. Harthacnut himself died in 1042 to be succeeded in England by a representative of the ancient West Saxon dynasty in the person of his half-brother, Edward the Confessor. The situation in Denmark itself remained intricate and difficult, and further complicated by the return in the mid-'40s to Northern politics of the charismatic figure of Harold Hardrada, St Olaf's half-brother, with great wealth from his service as captain of the Varangian Guard at Constantinople. The hopes of the Jelling dynasty were kept alive by the skilful and effective nephew of Cnut, Sweyn Estrithsson, the son of Cnut's sister. In 1047 King Magnus of Norway was killed in an accident. For the succeeding 17 years, a period of relative peace in English affairs under Edward the Confessor, the rivalries of the formidable Harold Hardrada and Sweyn were the dominant features of northern politics. Their rivalries merged into the great crisis that led to the Norman Conquest of England. Hardrada himself was killed at Stamford Bridge in September 1066. Sweyn continued to govern Denmark in his astute and capable fashion until his death in 1076. Intervention in English affairs brought material profit but no permanent gain in 1070 and 1071, though his heirs continued to harbour English ambitions until the assassination of St Cnut in 1086. Sweyn Estrithsson's outstanding contribution, however, lay not so much on the international scene as in his native Danish hearths. By the time of his death Denmark bore the stamp of a permanent Christian kingdom and the Viking days were virtually at an end.

Norway was more backward economically than Denmark and had more difficulties in achieving political shape. Communications overland were exceedingly difficult and there was – and long remained – a tendency for the three principal regions of Norway, the Trondelag, the western fjords, and the Vik, to develop their own independent characteristics, sometimes in conjunction with Danish or Swedish political support. The kings of the first Viking Age had established a firm tradition of Norwegian monarchy and a prince who aspired to wide authority was expected to have or to claim the blood of the Ynglinga, preferably direct descent from the prolific Harold Fairhair who died at a great age in 945. In the direct line Harold was succeeded by his son Eric Bloodaxe and then much more effectively – with Eric diverted to Viking and English adventures – by another of his sons, Haakon, foster-son of King Athelstan of

73

England. Drawing heavily from his English upbringing and experience Haakon proved himself worthy to rank among the select group of tenth-century rulers who were helping constructively to shape the permanent structure of the European polity. He had drawn up for him and his people codes of laws which were later elaborated into the laws of the Gulathing and Frostathing. He was responsible for exacting a form of military service based on the land, probably a modified form of the English *fyrd*. In religious matters, although a Christian himself, he did not attempt to convert the still heathen Norwegian peasantry. He died under attack from the Danish king, Harold Bluetooth, in 960, and was succeeded by Harold Greycloak, Haakon's nephew and the son of Eric Bloodaxe. Harold Greycloak, together with his brothers, had spent much of his early life in England and it is undoubtedly true that English religious and political influence had great impact on Norwegian affairs during this period. The impact was not altogether favourable. England itself under Edgar the Peaceful was reaching its height of development. Monarchical institutions were well advanced. The Church under the leadership of St Dunstan and the patronage of King Edgar was strong. The Benedictine revival was well under way and the relationship between king and Church symbolised in the impressive ceremony of royal coronation at Bath in 973. By that time Harold Greycloak was dead, killed in battle against the Danes at Limfjord. He left an unenviable reputation for harshness, mostly apparently because of his precocious attempts to suppress heathen practices. It may well be that the English wine of monarchy and Christianity was too heady for Norway at this stage: the German brew proved much more acceptable in the Danish kingdom.

The last 30 years of the tenth century were an unhappy time in Norwegian political life, heathen, weak, and divided in the face of Danish strength. In 995 Olaf Tryggvasson, a royal prince and one of the most colourful figures of the Viking Age, returned from a successful Viking raid on England, immensely wealthy and a zealous new convert to Christianity. He established himself in the north, in the Trondelag, and attempted to assert his kingship over all Norway. In England he had worked closely with the Danish king Sweyn Forkbeard, but now Sweyn proved too powerful and too adroit for him. Olaf died gallantly but in failure at the naval battle of Svöld in 1000, and Sweyn continued in essential command of Norwegian affairs. The conquest of England, 1013–16, by a curious quirk of fate brought Norway nearer realisation of independence. Sweyn died on campaign and his sons Harold and Cnut were both fully occupied in Danish and English affairs for some critical years. A young Norwegian prince, Olaf Haroldsson, representative of a south Norwegian branch of the Ynglinga, contended for the throne, defeated the Danish regent in a naval battle, and set himself up as king of Norway, 1016–26. He was a zealous Christian, a harsh reformer, and aroused enormous hostility among the conservative Norwegians. When Cnut had time enough he had little difficulty in overthrowing Olaf and Olaf's final attempt to regain his throne was defeated by the Norwegians themselves at the battle of Stiklestad in the Trondelag. His contribution to Norwegian unity proved, as we said above, greater in death than in life. Men forgot his harsh proselytising, his recruitment of Swedes and other non-Norwegian followers to further his ends, his taxes and his unpopularity. A cult quickly grew up around him. His epic and gallant death in a land battle (and all major political battles in recorded Norwegian history to this point had been sea battles) caused proliferation of legend. These legends, such was the temper of the time, became associated with miraculous cures from sickness, much of the apparatus that was needed to create a popular saint. The Church was quick to act when political circumstances were favourable and Olaf Haroldsson, known as Olaf the Stout, became St Olaf *perpetuus rex Norvegiae.*

Indeed it would be wrong to ignore the very real sentiments of national Norwegian feeling that were now apparent. After the death of Cnut in 1035 St Olaf's son, Magnus, was universally recognised as king in Norway. Such were the precarious circumstances of political life in the North that for a period in the 1040s he even found himself ruling the Danes as well. Under the astute Sweyn Estrithsson (1047–76) the Danes preserved their integrity and independence, but the Norwegians were now for a full generation the dominant political power in the North. Personal credit for this must go in part to Magnus, who left a good reputation as a legislator, and to the forceful Harold Hardrada who succeeded him on the Norwegian throne in 1047. These two rulers, of vastly different temperament and gifts, moulded the identity of historic Norway in the eleventh century. Under them and under Harold's son, Olaf Kyrre, the Peaceful (1066–93), the conversion to Christianity was completed and Norway accepted the pattern of traditional Western Christian monarchy. Harold Hardrada himself epitomises the changes that had come over the Northern scene in the two Viking centuries. A survivor of Stiklestad where he had fought as a 15-year-old boy by the side of his half-brother, King Olaf, he returned home wealthy and well renowned from service in the Varangian Guard in 1045 to share the throne with his nephew, Magnus. Much of the enormous energy of his full maturity went into schemes of Danish conquest at the expense of the often defeated but ever resilient Sweyn Estrithsson, and he died in his early 50s at the battle of Stamford Bridge, the oldest and most famous of his day of the contenders for the throne of England in 1066. His career, his name (hard-counsel), and his temperament bear many of the marks of the true Viking. But the contrast with the early Viking chiefs is also heavily marked. Harold Hardrada was a leader of national armies, a settled territorial king with ambitions to recreate the empire of Cnut, not a mere leader of Viking bands out for loot. Byzantine wealth and the profits of taxation lay more easily in his treasure chests than gold and silver from despoiled monasteries. He was a successor to King Olaf, a Christian king in his own strange Northern way. For Norway also the Viking Age was drifting towards its Christian end.

The mainland Norwegian story was complicated by the success of her colonising ventures in the northern islands, the Faroes, Iceland and Greenland. Iceland is far and away the best recorded of all the settlements. The outstanding Icelandic historian of the twelfth century, Ari the Learned, left a brief account, and the *Landnamabok* (or 'Book of Settlements') left a detailed description of the 400 or so chief settlers, 35 of whom had travelled in their own ships. Most were Norwegians from the western fjords or the Islands (it is said that Harold Fairhair, anxious in his days of so-called tyranny for the health of his beloved west and south-west imposed a tax on emigrants to Iceland) and there was also a Celtic element (strong from the Hebrides) which some place as high as 15%. By 930, when the population of Iceland consisted of at least 3,000–4,000 families, regular emigration came to an end, but contact remained a constant and important feature of tenth- and eleventh-century Norwegian life. The settlement flourished and at the end of the tenth century accepted Christianity, largely because of the enterprise and courage of Icelandic supporters of Olaf Tryggvasson.[3] The decision to accept the new faith was carefully debated and an Icelandic source gives an important insight into the nature of the acceptance which is helpful in relation to the whole story of the slow conversion and taming of the North. We are told that in 1000 A.D. (possibly 999):

It was then agreed by law that all should become Christians, and that all who were not baptized must become so; but certain ancient laws were retained, such as the practice of the exposure of children and the eating of horseflesh. Sacrifice in secret to the old gods was also permitted, but if witnessed by others incurred the sentence of banishment from the island for a period of three years. A few years later this relic of heathen practice was abolished.

The reaction provoked by the excessive zeal of a Harold Greycloak or Olaf Haroldsson in Norway was avoided and Iceland became a Christian community. Its first native bishop was consecrated by Adalbert of Bremen in 1056. Greenland had been settled from Iceland under the leadership of Eric the Red, and the Greenlanders accepted the Christian faith at the same time as the Icelanders. If their expeditions further west to Vinland and the American continent had achieved permanent success no doubt there, too, Christian churches would have been built early in the eleventh century. In this respect the outposts anticipated the homeland. The heavy hand of Olaf Tryggvasson proved oddly more effective at a discreet distance.

The history of Sweden from the middle of the tenth century to the end of the eleventh is obscure by the side of her western neighbours. Swedish interest in the expansion along the Russian waterway routes continued. Swedish merchants, sailors and soldiers found an outlet for their energies in opening up routes along the Volga into Central Asia and then later and more permanently along the Dnieper to Constantinople. In the course of the tenth century the fortified settlements along the waterways civilisation of Russia from Novgorod to Kiev became more Slav than Scandinavian, but Swedish enterprise and skill in navigation and trading still had a powerful influence on the development of early Russian communities. The route to Constantinople remained open for hardy traders and fighting men. It would be utterly misleading and inaccurate, however to suggest that Swedish interests lay exclusively to the east. For much of the early tenth century, during a period of Danish weakness, they had threatened to build up a kingdom, based on the trading wealth of Birka and of Hedeby in Schleswig that would incorporate a large part of southern Denmark together with Scania and the heartlands of the Uppsala kingdom into one political unit. There is even evidence of some Swedish settlement to be found in the place-name structure of Zealand itself. Such names were precocious and impermanent and did not survive the reassertion of Danish strength under Harold Bluetooth. The Swedes remained powerful on the waterways of the eastern Baltic. They controlled most of the islands, particularly Gotland where the settlement at Visby became an important element in the trading life of Scandinavia. The large number of English silver coins of the reign of Ethelred that have been discovered in Gotland testify to the importance of the site and also to the part played by the Swedes in Western affairs both directly and indirectly: they took their fair share of Danegeld. In Gotland itself, it has been pointed out that almost all coins found pre-dating 950 are Kufic and that the second half of the tenth century is when the German and English coins appear in force. In the hoards deposited between 990 and 1020 over 40 % of the coins were German and 10 % English but in the following 30 years 56 % were German, 30 % English and the Kufic contribution had dropped to a mere 5 %.[4] Memorial stones with runic inscriptions as well as the tangible evidence of coin hoards tell of their success in the later phases of Viking endeavour during the first half of the eleventh century. England is mentioned directly on no fewer than 25 rune stones, none earlier than *c.* 1000 A.D. We hear of a Viking named Ulf who received tribute three times in England, once from Toste (who may have been the leader of the Swedish contingent), once from Thorkell and once from Cnut himself. Others are said to have received tribute in England, some more than once. Their part in the Western enterprises of the Viking world was indeed far from negligible.[5] They did not provide the leadership, and there may be straightforward technical reasons for this. On the whole, their skills lay in the calmer waters of the Baltic and the Russian rivers. The special skills that went to make the sea-captains of the Atlantic were not theirs. On the other hand there were many Swedes among the ships' crews and more among the settlers in Norway, England, and Iceland than is often believed. Sweden, too, provided a ready home for exiles. Both in history and in saga it is common to find men who later contended successfully for Western thrones spending some years in exile among the Swedes. From time to time the Swedish political powers themselves intervened actively. The victory at sea in the battle of Svöld which resulted in 1000 in the death of Olaf Tryggvasson was a victory for the Swede, Olaf Skotkonung, the first known Christian king of Sweden. Olaf's son, Önund Jacob, rallied to support St Olaf of Norway in 1026 only to meet defeat at the hands of Cnut the Great. By and large, however, the Swedish kingdom seems something of a backwater throughout the period.

This impression is heightened when we look at the religious scene. There is an interesting parallel with the Norwegian situation where the colonies overseas accepted Christianity more decisively than the homeland. Strong Christian missionary efforts in the east led to the baptism of Vladimir, Grand Duke of Kiev, in 987, who – an early parallel to St Olaf of Norway – was recognised as a saint soon after his death in 1015. The Swedish kings accepted Christianity in the early eleventh century, but paganism was very strong, particularly around Uppsala. Even as late as the pontificate of Gregory VII in the 1070s a pagan temple still existed in use at Uppsala. The comparative weakness of the Swedish kingship is directly connected with the reluctance of the Swedish community to accept the new faith.

The contrast between Scandinavian history in the first and second Viking centuries is remarkable and significant. For the period that runs up to the mid-tenth century there is a mobility and uncertainty about Scandinavian affairs that is a true product of an age of migration. From mid-tenth century there is still much mobility and uncertainty, but the context is more cut and dried, more political. The main historical themes, as far as the homeland is concerned, deal with the consolidation of the monarchies and the acceptance of Christianity. Denmark is the earliest to be thoroughly Christianised. English missionaries played their part, but the main impetus was German, continental and indeed after 962 imperial. The north German sees were the active institutional agents, notably the see of Hamburg/Bremen. Norway was more slow-moving and cautious in its acceptance of Christianity. In the early stages English influence was paramount. Iceland was a special case. When organisation was needed – and Iceland in these respects as in all others retained its independence and peculiarities – it turned to Germany rather than England; but political accident, notably the great prestige of Hamburg/Bremen under Adalbert in the mid-eleventh century had much to do with this. Sweden was the last of the Scandinavian communities fully to accept Christianity. The strength of the ancient shrines at Uppsala reinforced its native conservatism, but there were also deep social reasons for the slowness of pace. Political life in Denmark and in Norway was unquestionably more mobile and hectic than in Sweden. The search for a monarchical solution to an overriding problem of law and authority prompted an acceptance of the traditional Western European answer. It is of amusing symbolic note that St Olaf's son, Magnus, who did so much to set the Norwegian monarchy on the right path, took his name from the second element of Charlemagne's name, *Carolus Magnus*. Denmark, Norway, and finally Sweden were brought squarely within the comity of Western monarchies.

By contrast the earlier Viking period seems much more primitive, epic and uncertain. Migration from 800 to 950 must have threatened at times to drain off not only the surplus but the heart and kernel of the native communities; just as the movements of the 4th and 5th centuries A.D. had left large tracts of potentially fertile land deserted. These threats were never realised, and the Scandinavian homelands themselves were ultimately (or so it seemed) strengthened by the colonising movements overseas. European conditions account in part for this. Feudal institutions, to the growth of which the stimulus of Viking attack in no small measure contributed, slowly brought peace and discipline to the Western world. The revival of the

German monarchy and the establishment of the Ottonian empire after 962 gave stability to the Germans, the north Italians, and the inhabitants of the old Middle Kingdom. Scandinavian traders, backed by the guarantee of good standing of Christian monarchs, were welcomed in imperial lands. Greater profit could now be made at infinitely less risk by peaceful traders than by violent looters. The lessons of the Viking Age had been slowly but thoroughly learned in the homelands. Skill at exacting taxes and maintaining permanent armies in communities that were predominantly aggressive had been acquired, notably from English sources. The first Christian Swedish king had the by-name 'Skotkunung', that is to say an exactor of *scot* or taxes. Yet one must not paint the picture in too peaceful and sedate a style. There were still murderous Vikings on the loose in the Western world late in the eleventh century. The impact of Scandinavian moves onto Britain 954–1087 was often as disastrous as in the earlier migration age. It mattered little to the dispossessed thegn or evicted *ceorl* that he suffered through the actions of national armies rather than murderous migrants. We shall now turn in the next chapter to a consideration of the extent and nature of this impact.

5.

The Course of the Scandinavian Invasions in England, *c.* 954–*c.* IIOO

It is not easy to put into proper perspective the relationship between Great Britain and the Scandinavians during this period. Strong Scandinavian settlements within the islands distort the picture. At times but not consistently these settlements themselves come to terms with the native inhabitants, at other times they are bitterly hostile. Differences between the Scandinavian communities were reflected in the British scene: the Norwegians tended to retain their individuality, their paganism and their ferocity longer than the Danes. In general it is true to say that we deal more with national armies on the move, with political seeking for power than in the earlier period; there is less of an urge for settlement and nothing of the nature of a migration. The tempo and importance of the movements vary among the British communities, and it is convenient to take them in turn, England, Wales, Scotland, and Ireland, while recognising the strong degree of interaction among the varying movements. It is generally true that the first generation of this period up to about 980 was a period of peace, that the subsequent 40 years was dominated by the Scandinavians with the greatest crises resolved between 1012 and 1016, and that the final half-century or so through to the death of William the Conqueror in 1087 saw a gradual though by no means inevitable or certain recession of Scandinavian pressure.

England demands pride of place in the narration because the maximum Scandinavian efforts in these islands were made on the whole successfully in the English direction. Under King Edgar the West Saxon monarchy had reached fresh heights and had finally been transformed into a monarchy of all England. Church and State were closely knit together. Full recognition had been given to the legal traditions of the Danelaw, but the Danish population settled in England were Christian and recognised the Christian king Edgar as their overlord. After the death of Edgar in 975, still a young man in his early 30s, dynastic weakness coupled with internal dissension partly attributable to the endowments and nature of the new Benedictine monasteries revealed flaws in the English political condition. Edgar's successor, Edward, the elder of his two surviving sons, was murdered in desperately suspicious circumstances that seemed to incriminate his own stepmother at Corfe Castle in Dorset. Her own son, Ethelred, succeeded his half-brother, to rule for the best part of 40 years over a kingdom fated to be savagely disrupted and finally conquered by Scandinavian hosts. Ethelred has not been fortunate in his historians, nor as far as one can judge, did he deserve to be. The contemporary Chronicler wrote at great length and detail about the campaigns of the early eleventh century. He clearly loathed Ethelred and was heavily inclined to attribute English disaster to lack of good faith, sheer treachery and perfidy, starting in the royal person and spreading throughout the body politic. *Ethel-ræd*, the noble counsel, became *Un-ræd* the no-counsel: a medieval ruler got the counsel he deserved! There were still good men in the kingdom, willing and anxious to carry on Edgar's traditions of government. Good law codes were issued. Techniques of administration and of government improved. The territorial courts of shires, hundreds, and boroughs were firmly established as part of the routine procedures of the land. This was the golden age of Anglo-Saxon prose, and Wulfstan, archbishop of York, 1002–23, and Aelfric, the homilist, of Eynsham and Cerne Abbas wrote splendid homilies and important treatises in the vernacular. Their note was consistently elegiac: the golden age politically lay in the past – in the reign of King Edgar. By the side of King Ethelred the reputation even of his harsh and unpleasant murdered half-brother flourished mightily. The young murdered king was regarded as a martyr and then as a saint; before the end of Ethelred's reign a special day of veneration was set aside for Edward, the Martyr. Anything was better than treacherous, womanising, incompetent Ethelred. England's collapse was a moral collapse, caused negatively by wavering loyalties and positively in Church and State by great treachery.

Record of renewed raiding begins in 980. Southampton was sacked and most of the citizens killed or taken captive, the Isle of Thanet ravaged, and Cheshire overrun by a strong naval force. In the following year the monastery at Padstow was destroyed and Devon and Cornwall heavily raided. In 982 Dorset and especially Portland suffered; and in the same year London was burnt down. There followed a lull in the record, if not in the harrying, until 988 when Watchet was attacked. An impression is given of probing attacks, some from the western seaboard, some from the north, by relatively small numbers of ships' crews, out for loot in treasure and slaves, possibly for their colonising ventures elsewhere west over sea. A major crisis occurred in 991. Earlier success, notably the sacking of London, whetted the appetite. Led by the Norwegian, Olaf Tryggvasson, and by two Danish captains, Jostein and Guthmund, a huge fleet, estimated at 93 ships, made a savage onslaught on the prosperous south-east. They attacked Folkestone, ravaged all around it, moved up the coast to Sandwich, and then – avoiding the Thames estuary – moved north to Ipswich, overran it all (presumably the south of Suffolk and north Essex), and advanced on Maldon. The defence of eastern England lay very much in the hands of two or three senior ealdormen, prominent among them ealdorman Brihtnoth who had been appointed to office as far back as 956 A.D. Brihtnoth led his army against the Vikings (a version of the Chronicle implies against Olaf specifically), but was defeated and killed. A contemporary epic poem of great skill and quality, one of the finest battle poems to be written in the English language, fills out the bare details of the Chronicle entry. We learn from it that Brihtnoth's army consisted of his hearth-troop and of the militia of the country-side whom he drew up in proper array, instructing them how they should stand and keep their ground and hold their weapons. Brihtnoth fought hard and after his death many of his hearth-troops performed their epic service, fighting to the last against increasing odds. The poet does not conceal the fact that Brihtnoth may have been over-rash in his pride in letting the Vikings come to grips instead of relying on his advantage in territory; nor does he deny that some cowards fled in their ingratitude. He succeeds in giving in superb poetry passages that express perfectly the loyalty that held the epic and the feudal world together. The old companion, Brihtwald, at the end of the battle, rallies the remnant of the hearth-troop:

> *Thoughts must be the braver, heart more valiant*
> *Courage the greater as our strength grows less.*
> *Here lies our lord, all cut down, the hero in the dust,*
> *Long may he mourn who thinks to turn from the battle play.*
> *I am old in years; I shall not turn hence,*
> *But by the side of the lord, the man I hold dear, I think to lie.*[1]

Lack of such loyalty brought disaster to Ethelred's realm, and the poet may already in 991 have been fully aware of it.

The poem also gives us valuable insight into the motives behind these renewed Viking attacks. The Vikings entered into negotiations with Brihtnoth, and their spokesman asked, before battle was joined, for 'treasure in return for peace', arguing that it would be better to buy off an attack with tribute rather than to suffer the onslaughts of such fierce men. In proper bullying fashion he argued that there was no need for them to destroy each other – provided that the English were rich enough. The Vikings were willing to make a truce in return for gold and he asked for wealth on their own terms, promising friendship and a peaceful departure in exchange for treasure. Brihtnoth contemptuously rejected the terms, but the poet clearly caught the echo of much English as well as Scandinavian sentiment when he framed the speech. One version of the Chronicle tells us that after the disaster at Maldon it was decided for the first time that tribute should be paid to the Danish men because of the great terror they were causing along the coast. Sigeric, archbishop of Canterbury, is said to have been the first to advise that course; and the first payment according to the Chronicle was the sum of £10,000. England was set on the course that was to prompt Kipling to write:

> *If once you have paid him the Danegeld*
> *You never get rid of the Dane.*

There has survived a copy of the treaty which King Ethelred and his counsellors made with the Viking leaders, Olaf Tryggvasson, Jostein, and Guthmund Steitasson.[2] It was probably made in 991 in direct consequence of the defeat at Maldon, though it is just possible that it was modified or brought up to date three years later when Archbishop Sigeric was still alive. The sum of money insisted on in relation to the truce was now £22,000 in gold and silver, and the purpose was the establishment of a general peace according to the terms made by Archbishop Sigeric, Aethelweard, ealdorman of Mercia, and Aelfric, ealdorman of East Anglia. The special concern of the treaty was to safeguard the lives and goods of peaceful traders who were Ethelred's subjects whether they were in English or foreign parts; and the Vikings pledged themselves to offer protection. Careful arrangements were also made to provide compensation and proper regulation of payments on a basis of equality between Englishmen and Danes, especially in trading settlements. No compensation was to be asked for slaughter and devastation before the treaty was made. If these indeed were the terms of the treaty of 991 their efficacy was not great. In 992 Ethelred assembled all the ships that were of any use at London, and made an attempt to trap the Danish fleet at sea. The plan was betrayed by Aelfric, the East Anglian ealdorman himself, a man Ethelred greatly trusted, and in the subsequent naval battle the English were soundly defeated. A similar story of betrayal was unfolded in the following year when the Danes sacked Bamborough and then turned south, ravaging both sides of the Humber estuary in Northumbria and Lindsey. The leaders of the English army summoned against them, Fræna, Godwin, and Frythegyst, were the first to lead the flight; and a later well-informed source adds the ominous information that they did so because they were Danes on their father's side.[3] It could be that the record of these years reveals attempts by a Scandinavian fleet to carry out the terms of the 991 treaty. Ealdorman Aelfric had been one of its guarantors and his desertion of Ethelred would be intelligible if he himself considered the king's plan to trap the enemy at sea treacherous and an infringement of the treaty. Ethelred's revenge was typically devious and ferocious: in 993 he captured the ealdorman's son and had him blinded.

This stage in the story of the Scandinavian invasions reached a fresh critical point in 994. In early September Olaf Tryggvasson returned to England in the company of no less a figure than Sweyn Forkbeard, king of Denmark. We are told that they came with 94 ships (it had been 93 in 991), and there is no reason to doubt the accuracy of the information. Systematic organisation is the hallmark of Sweyn's military enterprises: it is highly probable that the figures in the '90s indicate levies for a round 100 ships, the greater part of which made an active fleet of assault. The leading sea-captains of the Northern world in 994 were after a great prize. They launched their attack on London, and they were beaten off 'suffering more harm and injury than they ever thought any town-dwellers could do them.'[4] They recoiled all along the south-east, burning, ravaging, slaying everywhere along the coast, and in Essex, Kent, Sussex, and Hampshire. The interior did not escape. They seized horses and rode widely, continuing to do indescribable damage. The king and his councillors came to terms, promising them tribute and provisions in return for peace. The Scandinavians accepted the terms, took up winter quarters at Southampton, received supplies from all Wessex, and were paid £16,000 in cash. One event occurred that was of momentous consequence to Norwegian as well as to English history. Hostages were given to the fleet, and King Olaf was brought to Ethelred at Andover. There in the winter of 994–5 Olaf Tryggvasson was converted to Christianity. Ethelred was his sponsor at baptism, and bestowed great gifts on him; and we are told that he had been instructed in the faith by Aelfheah, bishop of Winchester. The conversion was genuine and deep. Olaf promised that he would not return to England in hostility; and he kept that promise.

85

After a lull of two years ravaging started again in 997, to continue almost without intermission for 20 of the most miserable years in English history. The chronicler who has left us a most graphic and detailed account of the events had no doubt whatsoever of the basic cause: lack of good leadership and consequent treachery and loss of morale. In his final recension of the annals for these years, probably prepared early in the reign of Cnut, he permitted himself occasional astringent asides which expressed his view of the general state of affairs. He does not condemn the policy of paying Danegeld, nor does he belittle the difficulties facing the English who were confronted by a ferociously mobile enemy in arrogant command of the seas with secure bases waiting for them not only in the Scandinavian homelands but in Ireland, the Isle of Man, the Scottish islands and – on at least one occasion – what the chronicler referred to as 'Richard's kingdom', that is to say the duchy of Normandy. He does condemn rightly the vacillations and deplorable lack of good timing in Ethelred's policy. He sums up his feelings in the annal for 1011. The Danes had overrun great tracts of eastern and southern England from the Wash through Oxfordshire to Hampshire and much of Wiltshire. 'All these disasters,' wrote the chronicler, 'befell us through bad policy, in that they were never offered tribute in time, nor fought against; but when they had done most to our injury, peace and truce were made against them; and for all this truce and tribute they journeyed none the less in bands everywhere, and harried our wretched people, and plundered and killed them'.[5] Where resolute leadership was given, as by the citizens of London from time to time, or by Ulfcetel, ealdorman of East Anglia, in 1004, or by Edmund Ironside, the Danes recoiled: looting and tribute-taking ceased to be profitable. As it was, for the greater part of the period they had the best of both worlds, much loot, easily come by, and fat tribute efficiently collected by the wealthy territorial government of Ethelred, No-counsel.

For England was undoubtedly wealthy and in some respects remarkably efficient. Vast sums were levied in tribute, and were collected: masses of silver pennies, the product of Danegeld as much as honest trade, have been discovered in Scandinavian lands, dating from the reign of Ethelred. Great efforts were expended, building and equipping massive fleets, but treachery, betrayal, sheer incompetence destroyed the best attempts at national defence. The English were consistently caught on the wrong foot, making immense efforts at the wrong place at the wrong time. The chronicler again brilliantly caught the mood of indecision and chaos in his account of the events of 1010:

86

Then they turned back to the ships with their booty. And when they were journeying to their ships, the English army should have come out again in case they wished to go inland. And when they were in the east, the English army was kept in the west, and when they were in the south, our army was in the north. Then all the councillors were summoned to the king, and it was then to be decided how this country should be defended. But even if anything was then decided, it did not last even a month. Finally there was no leader who would collect an army, but each fled as best he could, and in the end no shire would even help the next.

The course of the dismal narration up to the point of its final resolution with the victories of Sweyn Forkbeard and his son, Cnut the Great, is broken by two dramatic incidents of outstanding importance – the massacre of St Brice's Day in 1002 and the martyrdom of Aelfheah, archbishop of Canterbury, at Easter, 1012. Devastation in the West Country, notably at Tavistock in 997, was followed by further raiding in Dorset and Hampshire in the course of which the Danes discovered a convenient base in the Isle of Wight. Attempts to rally a naval force against them in Kent in 999 ended in miserable failure, and they ravaged and ravaged freely along the whole of the south coast in the opening years of the new century, especially Sussex (where they met hard resistance) and Devon. 1002 was a year of decisions, most would say of wrong decisions. Ethelred and his councillors attempted to buy off the raiders with massive Danegeld of £24,000. In the spring the English king married Emma, the daughter of the Norman duke. More confident, perhaps, now that friendly contact had been established with the Norman court, on St Brice's Day, 13 November, Ethelred perpetrated an infamous massacre of the Danes (the chronicler says 'all the Danish men who were in England') because he feared plots against his life and kingdom. The horror of the deed, at least in the southern part of the kingdom, is brought out by a charter relating to the monastery of St Frideswide in peaceful Oxford which renewed ancient privileges after the church and its charters had been burnt down during the massacre of the Danes. Reference is made to the royal decree that 'all the Danes who had sprung up in this island (sprouting like cockle among the wheat) were to be destroyed by a most just extermination'.[6] In Oxford the poor Danes had tried to save themselves by seeking sanctuary at St Frideswide's, breaking down the doors and bolts by force. Their pursuers had tried to force them out but had failed and in the ensuing tumult the church and its ornaments and its charters had been burned: no one thought to record whether the Danes also perished in the fire. Undoubtedly much passion was aroused in the south against the Danes. It was said later that Sweyn Forkbeard's own sister was killed during the massacre.

Sweyn certainly was in the forefront of the avenging force that burnt Norwich and Thetford in 1004. The stout resistance of the East Angles won some respite and a cruel famine in England still more but in 1006–7 a fearsome raid took place, and the English levies called out to protect the communities did as much damage as the Danes themselves. The Isle of Wight again provided a safe base for the Danish fleet in the autumn and the winter. The defences which since Alfred's day had made inland raiding hazardous had now cracked, and the Danes roamed about at will, even parading at Cuckamsley Barrow in defiance of the ancient proverb which had said that if ever they reached Cuckamsley they would never get back to the sea.[7] The chronicler made a special point of their arrogance in riding past the gates of Winchester to the sea, and commented that on this expedition they provided themselves with food and treasures from more than 50 miles from the sea. Ethelred's immediate answer was tribute and yet more tribute (he had spent Christmas safely with his food-rents in Shropshire): £36,000 was spent in 1007 alone. Even when he stirred himself to a sensible and systematic policy of shipbuilding the result was chaos, with one section of his fleet turning against another. A new Viking fleet, led by the Danish Viking, Thorkell the Tall, ravaged Kent, took great tribute, settled in their old harrying-headquarters, the Isle of Wight, and after a national effort against them had failed (thanks to the treachery of the sinister ealdorman, Eadric Streona) took up winter quarters on the Thames estuary, failing only against the determined resistance of the Londoners. The following years were years of disaster for the English with widespread raids from the Thames and East Anglia deep into English England: Oxford, Thetford, Cambridge, Bedford and Northampton all suffered specifically, and there was much harrying throughout Greater Wessex. The formidable East Anglian ealdorman, Ulfcetel, concentrated forces in Norfolk but they were defeated according to both English and later Norse poetic sources at Ringmere Heath.[8] The climax came in September 1011 when by treachery on an Englishman's part (Aelfmaer 'the archdeacon') Canterbury was captured and the archbishop himself taken prisoner. An immense tribute of £48,000 was levied, and all the chief councillors of England, ecclesiastical and lay, saw to it that it was paid after Easter. Meanwhile the archbishop's tragedy was played to its end. On the Saturday after Easter the Danish captors of the archbishop became very angry with him because he would not promise ransom (Florence of Worcester tells us that £3,000 was demanded); in their drunkenness – for they had got hold of wine from the south – they shamefully put him to death, pelting him with bones and ox-heads until one of their number, a recent convert named Thrum, put him out of his misery with a blow from the back of his axe. The fleet dispersed after the tribute had been paid, but Thorkell stayed on with a formidable company of 45 ships to act as a protector for the kingdom.

Affairs now quickly moved to their final resolution. Sweyn Forkbeard decided rightly that it was time again for his personal intervention. Accompanied by his young son, Cnut, he came with his fleet, probably in July 1013, to Sandwich, sailed north to the Humber, and then up the Trent to Gainsborough where he made his headquarters.

The *Encomium Emmae* in a near-contemporary account, admittedly as something of a rhetorical exercise, described the fleet in the following terms:

> When at last the soldiers were all assembled, they went on board the towered ships, each man having picked out by observation his own leader on the brazen prows. On one side lions moulded in gold were seen on the ships, on the other birds on the tops of the masts indicated by their movements the winds as they blew, or dragons of various kinds poured fire from their nostrils. Here there were glittering men of solid gold or silver almost like living people, there bulls, with arched necks and legs outstretched, were carved like real ones. . . . But why should I now dwell upon the sides of the ships, painted in bright colours and covered with gold and silver figures? The royal vessel excelled the others in beauty just as the king excelled the soldiers in the honour of his proper dignity, concerning which it is better for me to be silent than to speak inadequately. Placing their confidence in such a fleet, when the signal was suddenly given, they set out joyfully, and, as commanded placed themselves around the royal vessel, with steady prows, some in front and some behind. The blue water, smitten by many oars, might be seen foaming far and wide, and the sunlight, reflected in gleaming metal, gave out a doubled radiance.[9]

The Anglo-Scandinavians, Northumbrians, the men of Lindsey, the men of the Five Boroughs, and all the Danish settlers north of Watling Street, quickly submitted to him, giving hostages from every shire. Leaving the ships and hostages in the care of Cnut he advanced south, clearly treating Watling Street as something of a hostile frontier. Oxford and Winchester submitted. Only London held out, because King Ethelred and Thorkell were both inside the borough. Sweyn turned away to the west to Wallingford and then to Bath where all the western thegns submitted to him, giving hostages. Then he returned north to the ships where, as the chronicler tells us, all the nation regarded him as full king. At this point London capitulated and gave hostages because it was afraid he would destroy the city. Ethelred sent Queen Emma and their two sons, Alfred and Edward (the future Edward the Confessor) to Normandy. His own kingdom was virtually reduced to the area controlled by Thorkell's fleet which lay at Greenwich. Both Sweyn and Thorkell demanded payment and provisions for their troops in full. Ethelred then travelled the familiar Viking route to the Isle of Wight, spent Christmas there, and slipped across the Channel to exile in Normandy until the death of Sweyn on 3 February 1014 again transformed the political scene. Cnut stayed at Gainsborough until Easter, winning the support of the unfortunate people of Lindsey, but the English witan negotiated with the exiled Ethelred who promised just government, reform, and an amnesty for past deeds and words in return for wholehearted support without treachery. For once the English caught the Danes unawares. Cnut was forced to escape by sea, so betraying his Lindsey allies and leaving them to the far from tender mercies of the victorious English. He turned south to Sandwich, putting ashore there his hostages whom he caused to be savagely mutilated. But Ethelred was still forced to buy off a great army (presumably Thorkell's) at Greenwich with £21,000. Natural disaster, flood, the sickness of the king, and treachery undid the good work. Cnut was back ravaging in 1015 and forced the West Saxons into submission. Ethelred's son, Edmund Ironside, at long last, but too late, provided resolute leadership. An ugly war broke out that was quite different from earlier ventures. Men's loyalties were disturbed, and Cnut found unexpected support, even among the English. It was probably at this stage that the young Cnut accepted Christianity, and even before Ethelred's death on 23 April 1016, the Chronicle refers to him as *King* Cnut. The key to full political control was still London; and the loyalties of the Londoners were inclined to the old dynasty. Edmund Ironside led no fewer than five full-scale national expeditions against Cnut in the course of 1016. The final battle came on 18 October at Ashingdon in Essex. Thanks to the now familiar treachery of ealdorman Eadric who, with his men from Herefordshire, was the first to turn in flight, Cnut won a great victory: the bishop of Dorchester, the abbot of Ramsey, three ealdormen and the son of the East Anglian ealdorman were killed 'and all the nobility of England'. Edmund was still formidable in defeat. The two kings met at Olney, near Deerhurst, and agreed on a partition, Edmund to succeed to Wessex, and Cnut to Mercia and the Danelaw. The Londoners were at last forced to make what was virtually a separate peace, and the Danes took up winter quarters inside the city. Before the terms of the agreement could be tested Edmund died on 30 November 1016. Cnut succeeded with common consent and through universal exhaustion to the whole kingdom. At some time late in Ethelred's reign (probably in the dark year 1014 which he himself described as the year when the Danes persecuted the English the most), Wulfstan, archbishop of York preached a powerful homily, the so-called *Sermo Lupi ad Anglos,* the sermon of 'Lupus' (Wulfstan) to the English, which clearly had great impact on the learned opinion of the day.[10] In it he arraigned the English for their wickedness, their impiety, and above all for their lack of loyalty to their kindred and to their lords. He was grievously concerned not only about the obvious evil consequences of Viking attack, but about the breakdown in social order which seemed to be resulting from it. In a great rhetorical passage which deserves quotation in full he conveys admirably the sense of shame and misery which many English Christians must have felt:

And lo! how can greater shame befall men through God's anger than often does us for our own deserts? Though any slave runs away from his master and, deserting Christianity, becomes a viking, and after that it comes about that a conflict takes place between thegn and slave, if the slave slays the thegn, no wergild is paid to any of his kindred; but if the thegn slays the slave whom he owned before, he shall pay the price of a thegn. Very base laws and shameful tributes are common among us, through God's anger, let him understand it who can; and many misfortunes befall this people again and again. Things have not gone well now for a long time at home or abroad, but there has been devastation and persecution in every district again and again, and the English have been for a long time now completely defeated and too greatly disheartened through God's anger; and the pirates so strong with God's consent that often in battle one puts to flight ten, and sometimes less, sometimes more, all because of our sins. And often ten or a dozen, one after another, insult disgracefully the thegn's wife, and sometimes his daughter or near kinswoman, whilst he looks on, who considered himself brave and mighty and stout enough before that happened. And often a slave binds very fast the thegn who previously was his master and makes him into a slave through God's anger. Alas for the misery, and alas for the public shame which the English now have, all through God's anger. Often two seamen, or maybe three, drive the droves of Christian men from sea to sea, out through this people, huddled together, as a public shame for us all, if we could seriously and rightly feel any shame. But all the insult which we often suffer we repay with honouring those who insult us; we pay them continually and they humiliate us daily; they ravage and they burn, plunder and rob and carry on board; and lo, what else is there in all these events except God's anger clear and visible over this people?

It is clear that the most ambitious of the Scandinavian leaders who worked for a favourable settlement did not themselves wish to overwhelm the social order. Wulfstan quickly became the most trusted adviser in legal matters to Cnut. Experience as archbishop of Anglo-Scandinavian York in the early eleventh century (as in the late 9th) was no negligible political asset.

Cnut's victories were followed by a period sometimes known as the Danish interlude in English political history, a quarter of a century during which the descendants of Gorm the Old occupied the English throne. The surviving princes of the legitimate West Saxon dynasty were exiled, some to Normandy and others (the children of Edmund Ironside) to the Empire and ultimately to Hungary. Cnut had learned many lessons from his campaigns in England, among them the need to reconcile the Danes and the English, and to use Christianity as a means to that end. In quite startling fashion he ordered Emma, Ethelred's widow, to be fetched from Normandy to be his wife. She obeyed and, right through to her death in 1052, the 'Lady of Winchester', wife to two kings of England and mother to two more, exercised great political influence on events in England. Cnut laid an enormous tribute, £72,000, on all England, and exacted a further £10,500 from London alone. He came to an agreement with some of the most prominent advisers to Ethelred, notably with Wulfstan who drafted Cnut's English laws for him. At Oxford in 1018 Cnut caused to be drawn up a code of laws in the full succession to the laws of Edgar (his conscious model) and those of Ethelred: this was a deliberate act of reconciliation. The councillors promised that 'above all things they would honour one God and steadfastly hold one Christian faith, and would love King Cnut with due loyalty and zealously observe Edgar's laws'.[11] This was a strange metamorphosis into a Christian king for the young, savage and probably scared barbarian prince who had mutilated and maimed his English hostages in 1014. In 1019 Cnut returned to Denmark to ensure that his claim to succeed his brother on the Danish throne was not questioned, but he returned to England in the following year, and England continued to be at the centre of his multifarious interests for the rest of his life. He reasserted again his will that all the nation should observe the laws of King Edgar in a letter which he appears to have sent from Denmark in late 1019 or early 1020 before his personal return.[12] It is strongly ecclesiastical in tone and was addresssed to his archbishops and bishops as well as to Earl Thorkell (the Tall) who acted as regent in his absence and to the other earls. God's law was placed on the same footing as Cnut's royal authority and other secular law; and Thorkell was expressly enjoined to cause evil-doers, who acted in defiance of such properly constituted authorities, to do right. There is a significant reference also in this letter to messages from the Pope at Rome. Cnut's public image in England was consistently to represent the fervour of the convert, more Christian than the Christians, more true a representative of the Christian kingship of Edgar than Edgar's own blood descendants. The image was probably near the truth. Cnut was, as we have seen, a strong king of Denmark. He was heavily involved in Northern politics. He acted on occasion with true Viking violence. The treacherous Eadric Streona and other Englishmen he could not trust did not survive his accession a twelvemonth. His marriage customs were Danish rather than Western Christian. But Cnut like so many of his Scandinavian contemporaries accepted thoroughly the organisation and the basic teachings of the Christian Church, and had less trouble than most – particularly those of his Norwegian contemporaries – in rejecting ancient pagan beliefs. One of the best remembered acts of his early reign in England was the solemn translation of the relics of the martyred archbishop, Aelfheah, from London to Canterbury in June 1023, in the presence of the king himself, of Queen Emma, and of their royal child, Harthacnut.

The *Encomium Emmae* gives in its typical rhetorical manner an indication of contemporary reaction when it describes Cnut's visits to the abbeys of St Omer and St Bertin:

> When Canute entered the monasteries and had been received with great honour, he advanced humbly and prayed with complete concentration and wonderful reverence for the intercession of the saints, his eyes fixed on the ground and overflowing with a veritable river of tears. And when the time came for heaping the altars with royal offerings, how often did he first press kisses with tears on the

pavement! how often did self-inflicted blows punish that reverent breast! what sighs he gave! how often did he pray that the heavenly mercy should not disdain him! At length at his request his offering was supplied to him by his followers, no one, nor such that could be enclosed in a purse, but a man brought it, something very large, in the ample folds of his cloak, and this the king placed on the altar with his own hands, a cheerful giver according to the apostolic admonition. But why do I say altar when I remember seeing him going round every corner of the monasteries and passing no altar, however small, without giving a gift and pressing a sweet kiss on it?[13]

Cnut spent most of the early years of the 1020s in England, entrusting much of his royal interest in Denmark to the care of the powerful earl Ulf, Cnut's own brother-in-law. There was good practical reason for this concern. England was far and away the wealthiest part of his domains, and Cnut wanted to set up the governing machinery, particularly the tax-collecting machinery in Church and State, on a firm footing. He succeeded, and his success contributed greatly to further success in Scandinavia itself. Scandinavian historiography naturally tends to concentrate on the attempts of St Olaf to build up a permanent kingdom for himself in Norway. Later poetic authorities tell us of much bribery and subornation on Cnut's part, all of which may be attributed to his control of English wealth. The political and military lines, as we have seen, are shadowy. A great battle at the Holy River probably in 1026 was indecisive in the sense that the three Scandinavian rulers all recoiled on their own kingdoms, though the Anglo-Saxon Chronicle hints at near disaster for Cnut when it records that 'many many on king Cnut's side were destroyed, both Danish and English men, and the Swedes had control of the field'. Earl Ulf who had betrayed Cnut was the one to suffer personally: the king had him murdered in Roskilde church – and saw to it that generous compensation was paid to the earl's widow, Cnut's own sister. English money constantly undermined Olaf's position in Norway. In 1028 Cnut went from England to Norway, drove Olaf from the land, and made good his claim to Norway. When Olaf returned in 1030, the Anglo-Saxon Chronicle recounted simply yet comprehensively, 'he was killed in Norway by his own people and was afterwards holy'.[14]

The late 1020s provided Cnut with an opportunity to act on an international stage. After the battle of Holy River he felt secure enough to make a journey to Rome for the imperial coronation of the emperor Conrad II. On his way back to Denmark he wrote a remarkable letter to the archbishops, bishops and all the leading men of England, reporting on the practical results of his visit and telling of his intention to visit England as early in the summer as he could get a fleet equipped. Cnut had been well received by both the Pope and the emperor. He had been most impressed with Rome, and the emperor had showered gifts and presents on him, vessels of gold and silver and silk robes and costly garments. There was a business side to the visit as well as a social. Cnut had arranged favourable tolls through imperial and especially through Burgundian land, and had also safeguarded his archbishops from the excessive extortions imposed on them at the papal court which they visited when they received their *pallia*. He exhorted his councillors to maintain just laws and his bishops and reeves to see to the detailed collection of taxes and dues. He explained that he had to go to Denmark first to conclude a firm treaty with the peoples and communities which had opposed him and to set in order and pacify his kingdom 'here in the east'. The remarkable feature of the letter is indeed its very Englishness. Cnut styled himself, accurately enough, 'king of all England, and of Denmark, and of the Norwegians, and of part of the Swedes'. Scandinavians could do well for themselves in England and at least one later bishop of Lund (who had also been a bishop in the Orkneys) had been happy to act as a keeper of the king's treasure in England; this letter confirms the general feeling that England was central to Cnut's territorial, financial, and personal interests.[15]

Cnut was not unmindful of his wider Scandinavian duties and obligations and as early as 1023 sent his young son Harthacnut to Denmark, presumably with the view to having him brought up as a prince fully acceptable to the Danish people. After the death of St Olaf Cnut was universally recognised in Norway, but his experiments at remote government were not happy. He relied on his wife, *more Danico*, Aelfgifu of Northampton and their son Sweyn to act as resident regents for them, and they both built up a well of hatred for the oppressive Dane within the Norwegian kingdom. Scotland submitted to his authority in 1031 and Wales, too, appears to have recognised his lordship. The encomiast of his wife, Emma, described Cnut as emperor of five kingdoms.[16] He died at Shaftesbury on 12 November 1035, still a young man, and was buried at Winchester. He had been king of all England for nearly 20 years. He had given England peace and prosperity, above all freedom from savage raiding, after the horrors and devastation of the reign of Ethelred. Evidence of possible slighting of fortifications at Cricklade and Cadbury may well indicate the confidence of the new régime at least in Wessex under Cnut and Earl Godwin.

Fear of a repetition of the disasters of the opening years of the century probably contributed to the curious set of political compromises reached in England during the seven years after Cnut's death. Harthacnut succeeded to Denmark and St Olaf's son, Magnus, entered his Norwegian inheritance. Tensions erupting into open conflict between Denmark and Norway helped to ease the pressure in England. The original intention was almost certainly that Harthacnut should enter the joint inheritance of Denmark and England, but political circumstances determined otherwise. Aelfgifu of Northampton had proved a disastrous regent in Norway. She and her son, Sweyn, were expelled; for a short while Sweyn shared authority in Denmark with Harthacnut but he died before the plausibility of the arrangement could be properly tested. Aelfgifu had another son, Harold Harefoot, who claimed also to be Cnut's son. He proved to have a substantial following in England and in 1036 Leofric, earl of Mercia, the northern thegns and, most significantly of all, the shipmen in London, chose him to be regent for himself and his brother Harthacnut. This act opened up an ancient political division in England. Harthacnut's mother, Queen Emma, supported by Godwin, earl of Wessex, championed her son's cause, but in the end had to compromise. She was left in possession of her beloved Winchester, her son's hearth-troop and – through the loyalty of Godwin – the earldom of Wessex. This was a temporary unsatisfactory arrangement as a result of which occurred one of the great tragedies of pre-Conquest history. Ethelred's two young sons by Emma, Edward and Alfred, had long been in exile in Normandy. The younger of them, Alfred, now came to England, wishing to join his mother, Emma, at Winchester. Godwin played a devious game, captured the young prince, cruelly treated his followers, and betrayed him to Harold Harefoot who had him blinded so savagely that he died of his wounds in the care of the monks of Ely. The chronicler says that 'no more horrible deed was done in this land since the Danes came' and much of the bad blood between the Godwin family and Edward the Confessor, Prince Alfred's full brother and companion in exile, has indeed been attributed to this incident.

Emma herself was unable to keep together the forces loyal to Harthacnut (he was 'too long in Denmark') and in 1037 Harold Harefoot was chosen everywhere as king in spite of all the doubt over his paternity. Support from the fleet coupled with a deep desire to avoid civil war decided the issue in his favour. Emma was forced into exile, choosing this time to go to her kinsfolk at Bruges in face of the disturbed politics in Normandy. When Harold died at

Oxford on 17 March 1040 it was to Bruges that messengers were sent, asking Harthacnut to claim his inheritance. He arrived at Sandwich in June and was well received by Englishmen and Danes. Emma returned also, and in the following year her surviving son, Edward, was summoned from Normandy to share the throne with his young half-brother. This recall of the prince of the old royal stock is the only action the chronicler finds to praise in Harthacnut: otherwise all is complaint over taxation for the upkeep of the navy and the army, for oppressive measures in collecting taxation, and in acts of revenge and treachery Harthacnut even had the body of Harold Harefoot dug up and thrown in the fen. When he died 'as he was standing at his drink' on 8 June 1042 all the people chose Edward as king in London – and one chronicler added 'as was his natural right'.[17]

One thread through the political tangle was the desire to avoid civil war, and this same desire helped Edward, in spite of his lack of obvious warlike qualities, to keep his throne in peace for nearly a quarter of a century. Another thread was the existence of a peace-keeping navy, probably originally Thorkell the Tall's creation, but brought into the status of a permanent institution by Cnut. A third and possibly decisive thread was the concern of Denmark and Norway with their own affairs, part of the painful process of growing to nationhood. In making his successful bid for the English throne Harthacnut lost control of Danish affairs, and Magnus Olafsson of Norway was effective ruler of Denmark for the greater part of the 1040s until Sweyn, son of the murdered earl Ulf and of Cnut's sister, Estrith, won his skilful way to his uncle's Danish heritage. By the spring of 1050 Edward was confident enough to pay off nine of the 14 ships which he had kept as a standing fleet (in itself a substantial reduction from Cnut's day) and offer only a year's contract to the remainder. Peace had brought some relief to the burden of taxation that had seemed to support the fleet. Viking raids still continued but were spasmodic local affairs, often under-taken from western Britain, Ireland or the Isle of Man. A very heavy raid, briefly and ineptly mentioned in the Anglo-Saxon Chronicle, led by the Norwegian king's son, Magnus Haroldsson, took place in 1058.[18] Both the Norwegian king, Harold Hardrada, and the Danish king, Sweyn Estrithsson and his successors retained interest in the English crown. As a fitting end to the Viking story a word should be said about the ambition of both these men; although it must be recognised that their ambitions have less of the Viking and more of the established political leader to them.

Harold Hardrada, 'hard-counsel', governed Norway strongly for nearly 20 years. He remained a great captain of fighting men right to the end. By the terms of an agreement made between his nephew Magnus Olafsson and Harthacnut he had inherited some claim to the English succession. He was political realist enough to know that the claim could not be substantiated initially and concentrated instead on Dano-Norwegian affairs. There he achieved military and naval success and the part fulfilment of political ambition. He consolidated his hold on the Norwegian kingdom but made no effective political headway in Denmark itself. Even so he had reason to be pleased with himself; by the early 1060s there was no immediate danger of a political split along the lines of weakness that divided the three major divisions of Norway. The Vik was becoming as integral a part of Norway as Nidaros itself. The golden moment for English adventure came in 1065–6 in the last years of the Confessor's reign and during the brief troubled reign of his successor. Cnut had relied greatly on a new class of earl, possessing immense regional authority, to buttress up royal power. Godwin, earl of Wessex from Cnut's early days to his death in 1053, was the most influential of the earls, so much so that the Confessor had forced him and his sons into exile from autumn 1051 to 1052. He returned, possibly on terms, but with little diminution of strength, and his sons inherited and extended his offices and ability. The eldest survivor of the sons, Harold Godwinsson, was married to the king's sister, succeeded to the earldom of Wessex, and built up a military reputation second to none in England. By the time of Edward's death early in 1066 Harold was the strongest man in the kingdom, regarded by many as the natural successor to the old king. Harold's younger brother Tostig governed the earldom of Northumbria harshly for a whole decade, from 1055 to 1065. His harshness brought retribution and revolt. The men of Northumbria rose against him, forced his flight south and ultimate withdrawal to Flanders, bitterly disappointed at the lack of support from his brother Harold. From the storm-centre at Flanders spread a whole network of intrigue that was finally to result in the Norman Conquest of England.

Harold Godwinsson was acclaimed king on Edward's death in early 1066. By early summer Tostig was already harrying the east coast, on the whole unsuccessfully but probably content in the knowledge that he had the support of the Norwegian king. The men of the Scottish Isles also enter the tangled story of intrigue about this time and it is hard to believe that William of Normandy did not have a very good idea of activities in northern waters. Tostig himself protested that his ambition was limited to the recovery of his earldom of Northumbria, but the other men were playing for higher stakes.

The sheer size of Hardrada's intervention, coming as it did in September, must have come as a shock to the north of England. Reinforced by the earl of Orkney and his men, as well as by Tostig, his fleet is said to have included 300 ships and to have been manned by at least 9,000 men. After preliminary skirmishes on the coast in Cleveland, Scarborough and Holderness the main effort was made at the traditional point of weakness in the Humber estuary. His objective was York. The northern earls, Edwin and his brother Morcar (Tostig's successor to Northumbria), fought bravely but were defeated at Fulford Gate on the Ouse, two miles south of York, on Wednesday 20 September. The Scandinavians entered York peacefully, enlisting support for what Harold now proclaimed his true purpose, the conquest of England. The ravaging Viking of Scarborough was already turning into the statesman king of York. He withdrew eight miles to Stamford Bridge in what seems in retrospect to have been a somewhat over-confident and relaxed frame of mind, prepared to receive hostages from the whole of Yorkshire. Instead he received Harold Godwinsson and his English army which in one of the epic forced marches of Northern history moved from its role as guardian of the southern shires to cope with this sudden and devastating menace from the north. On Monday, 25 September, Harold Godwinsson caught the invaders far from their ships, with a vital bridge inadequately guarded, generally unprepared for a major attack. Later legend made up for hard fact in poetic and historical accounts of the battles. The confrontation of the two kings, Harold of England and Harold of Norway, was made all the more poignant by the quarrel between the sons of Godwin: the promise to Harold of seven feet of English ground because he is larger than other men, Harold's grudging admiration for his rival ('a small man but he stands well in his stirrups'), and the final irony that William the Norman was the ultimate beneficiary of the holocaust in the north all served to feed the poetic imagination – and possibly to give an occasional glimpse of poetic truth. A late addition to one manuscript of the Anglo-Saxon Chronicle tells of the epic last fight of one Norwegian hero who tried to stem the English advance across the fatal bridge.[19] The known facts bring out the completeness of the victory. A couple of dozen ships were enough to take the survivors back to the islands and the North. Harold Hardrada and Tostig both met death on the field of battle. Harold was generous to the ultimate survivors. He permitted Olaf, Harold's son, and the earl of Orkney to depart in peace with the pitiful remnant.

This was a fortunate piece of statesmanship for the English.

Olaf succeeded to the Norwegian kingdom and turned out to be one of the most peaceful of medieval Norwegian rulers, well earning his name of Olaf Kyrre, the peaceable. We hear of occasional Norwegian raids, usually operating along the west coast through the northern and western isles in the following century. The Viking Age in England ended as far as the Norwegians were concerned with the death of Harold Hardrada at Stamford Bridge.

English victory at Stamford Bridge was followed within the space of three weeks by devastating defeat at Hastings on Saturday, 14 October 1066. This is only remotely a Viking venture and not within our terms of reference. There remains the Danish side of things to be considered. Sweyn Estrithsson was Cnut's nephew and as such far from disinterested in English ventures. In 1066, however, he seems to have given some support to William of Normandy. His main delight was surely that the massive fleet prepared by Harold Hardrada turned west over sea rather than south against the Danish homelands. When William's settlement of England ran into its early and greatest crisis 1069–71, Sweyn judged the time ripe for intervention. The gravest peril to William came at York and the earldom of Northumbria and in the Fenlands of East Anglia and Cambridgeshire. Danish fleets were present off both areas, and more resolute leadership might have turned the balance, particularly during the rebellion of Hereward in the Isle of Ely. Instead the Danes permitted themselves to be bought off, rebellion was quelled in typical Norman fashion, piecemeal and harshly, and the last serious opportunity of a lasting Anglo-Danish kingdom was lost. One further effort was made under Sweyn's successor in 1085. It was a serious enough threat for William to stir his administrative and military advisers to maximum effort. The chronicler tells us that a greater force of Frenchmen was recruited on this occasion than men had ever seen before in England; and the need to provision them properly may have been one of the immediate reasons for the gigantic survey of the English kingdom which resulted in the production of Domesday Book. The murder of the Danish king Cnut Sweynsson brought an end to the threat. Contact between the two kingdoms was not lost. Traders from Scandinavia continued to be received on favourable terms along the eastern seaboard. London continued to offer privileges to Danish merchants.[20] But England was brought securely by its Norman king-dukes into the Gallic Romanic orbit. The feudal settlement proved an effective safeguard against external attack as well as against internal disruption. To raid England ceased to be profitable and from Denmark as well as from Norway the threat of a political conquest disappeared. The Normans may indeed have plundered their subjects. They certainly protected them from others; and England passed out of the Scandinavian political orbit.

6.

The Course of the Scandinavian Invasions in Wales, Ireland, Scotland and the Isles, c. 954–c. 1100

Wales

The middle of the tenth century marks the end of an important phase in Welsh political history, and the beginning of a new chapter in the story of her contacts with the Vikings. Wales had weathered the first Scandinavian onslaughts exceedingly well. Alone of the principal political units of Britain, Wales had avoided yielding substantial tracts of territory to Scandinavian adventurers. There were no significant territorial settlements made in the country. Credit for this remarkable achievement must go chiefly to the political leadership first of Rhodri the Great (844–78) and then of Hywel Dda (c. 926–50). Rhodri had been killed by the English but his successors, and especially his grandson Hywel, worked very closely with their English fellow-Christians against the heathen Danes. There was a positive lull in Scandinavian activity in Wales in the second quarter of the tenth century, a lull which may also be associated with indications of Danish presence in Brittany between 920 and 940. Hywel's death in 950 was followed however by a disastrous period of civil dissension and raids from overseas. Unfortunately records are very brief and unsatisfying, no more than single line entries in annals or incidental embroidery to lives of saints and ecclesiastical histories of a later period. Enough has remained to suggest some possible generalisations about the raids. The vast majority depended directly upon Scandinavian settlers in easy sailing distance from the Welsh shores, the men of Dublin, or other Irish settlements, men from the Isle of Man or the Hebrides. Occasional raiding parties came direct from the Northern Isles or even from the Scandinavian homeland, for all of which there is record from Norway and none from Denmark. Even then to these raiders Welsh ventures were secondary, almost incidental and accidental: their main objectives lay elsewhere along the seaboard or deep into England. There was no systematic purpose behind the enterprises of the type only too obvious in English affairs during the reign of Ethelred. Scandinavian attacks on Wales were more Viking in the traditional sense than were Scandinavian attacks on England. Loot, especially silver and easily won treasures from monasteries of easy access, was the prime aim. There was some use made of Scandinavian seamen as mercenaries by Welsh princes myopically concerned with their own internecine conflicts. Maredudd ab Owain (986–99), powerful ruler of Deheubarth, who had himself used Scandinavian mercenaries, was compelled to pay a penny a head in order to redeem Welsh prisoners at the height of the Norse attacks.[1] For many Vikings Wales offered no more than a little profitable sport on the way to English ventures. On occasion nevertheless, as we shall see later when we come to examine the nature of the permanent impress of Scandinavians on the British communities, there is evidence which may suggest a somewhat different attitude, possibly connected with attempts to establish permanent bases in Wales, both North and South, as a means of servicing traders to Chester and to Bristol.

In the half-century that followed the death of Hywel Dda specific record has survived of some 14 or 15 severe raids, mostly on Dyfed and the Bristol Channel and on Anglesey and the Lleyn peninsula. Where a place of origin for the raiding fleets is specified, Dublin and the Isle of Man often appear. Olaf Cuaran (945–80) of Dublin and his sons and a Scandinavian dynasty established in the Isle of Man were the principal and natural leaders of such expeditions. Monasteries were, as always, vulnerable: in the year 988 St David's, Llanbadarn Fawr, St Dogmaels, Llanilltud and Llancarfan all suffered. St David's indeed was sacked no fewer than three times in the last 20 years of the century (982, 988 and 999) and on the last occasion, in an incident which caught the imagination of contemporaries and of later generations, Bishop Morgeneu was killed in the course of the raid. Two centuries later the bishop's death was read as just retribution for his laxness in rejecting the ascetic observances proper to his degree: 'because he ate flesh he became flesh'.[2] The ancient kingdom of Gwynedd suffered severely from its proximity to the raiders' headquarters. Successful attacks were made on Holyhead (961), Towyn (963), Penmon (971), and Clynnog (978), as well as more generalised attacks on Anglesey which at times seem to have been threatened with a more permanent conquest. Bede had long ago referred to the Isle of Man and Anglesey (Môn) as the Menevian islands, and there was a natural link between the two. Any political power in the Isle of Man enjoying command of the sea, would find a convenient outlet in the direction of Anglesey, very exposed and vulnerable to resolute attack from the sea. Aberffraw on its west coast, the princely headquarters, had been thoroughly sacked as early as 968. Magnus Haroldsson, the leader of the Vikings, settled on the Isle of Man, raided Penmon in 971 and his brother, Godfrey Haroldsson (who succeeded Magnus in 977) conducted four recorded full-scale expeditions, three of which, in 972, 980 and 987, were directed specifically against Anglesey. In 972 Godfrey made himself temporarily master of the island, and it could well be that he was looking in his brother's lifetime for a more independent principality of his own. If he had such ambitions they were not realised, as his later career clearly demonstrates. He became lord of the Isle of Man and almost archetypal Viking raider. The last of his Anglesey expeditions was recorded in Irish annals as well as in Welsh. It seems to have been exceptionally ferocious and also exceptionally profitable. It is said that 1,000 Welshmen were killed in this campaign and 2,000 captives taken, presumably into slavery.[3]

Wales played little part in the series of crises that racked the English realm during the reign of Ethelred, much less so than during the Alfredian period. Sea communications remained open and vigorous with Ireland, and indeed the outstanding feature of the eleventh century in the west was the slow growth of an Irish Sea political circle in which the old identities of Scandinavian and Celt were blurred. Exiles from Ireland found refuge in Wales and exiles from Wales found refuge in Ireland. Gruffydd ap Cynan, the ruler of Gwynedd from 1075 (with interruptions) to his death in 1137, was said to have been born in exile in Dublin in 1054 or 1055 and brought up within the Scandinavian settlement there.[4] Raids still continued well into the late eleventh century, but became increasingly incidental, irritants rather than serious political forces. Pressure from the east (successfully resisted by the north Welsh prince of Gwynedd, Gruffydd ap Llewelyn, until he was overwhelmed by Harold Godwinsson in 1063) was the dominant political issue, exaggerated and exacerbated by the Norman Conquest. A Norwegian fleet, led by Magnus, son of Harold Hardrada, had helped Gruffydd ap Llywelyn in 1058, probably in the course of testing the temperature of the English political situation. The new Norman earls of Hereford (to 1076), Shrewsbury, and Chester provided the central political interest as they supported Norman lords in their movements west. The end of the true Viking intervention in Wales comes in relation to the Norman earl of Chester towards the end of the century. Early Norman successes met with stiffening resistance in north Wales. Hugh Lupus, earl of Chester, accompanied by Hugh Montgomery, earl of Shrewsbury, made a decisive effort to master the north in 1098. The native Welsh princes withdrew to Anglesey, relying on a fleet of Scandinavian-Irish mercenaries for support in their island fastness. The mercenaries proved treacherous, and Gruffydd ap Cynan fled to Ireland. Anglesey was ravaged by the Normans and the conquest seemed complete when a Norwegian fleet, commanded by Magnus Barefoot, king of Norway, appeared off Priestholm. In the ensuing battle the earl of Shrewsbury was killed, possibly by the Norwegian king himself, and the extreme precariousness of their hold on Anglesey made evident to the Normans. The Norwegian fleet withdrew, but so did the Normans. No further systematic attempt to conquer Wales west of Conway was to be made for many generations. This last intrusion of Viking power into Welsh affairs typifies the contact of Scandinavians with Wales: incidental, mysterious, ferocious, and of fringe importance. Contact with Ireland was another matter.

Ireland

In Ireland too the middle of the tenth century witnessed the beginning of an important stage in the history of the island. From 920–50 the history of the Scandinavian settlement at Dublin had been closely linked with attempts to create a joint kingdom of Dublin and York. Olaf Sihtricson, better known as Olaf Cuaran, twice established himself as king at York, but in 952 finally gave up his Northumbrian ambitions and resumed his kingship at Dublin. For close on 30 years he ruled the Scandinavian colony there vigorously and with considerable success. Relationships with the native Irish were mixed. He married an Irish princess himself with the result that his sons could draw on loyalties from both communities. He was converted to Christianity and treated with the other political powers of Ireland as one of a permanent group: there was little feeling of intrusion or of ephemeral nature about the Scandinavians in Dublin at this stage. When in 980 his sons were defeated in battle at Tara by the Irish high king, Olaf fled the country and died as a simple Christian pilgrim on the island of Iona. He was succeeded by his son, Gluniarainn (Iron Knee), who allied with his Irish kinsman (and victor) the high king Mael Sechlainn (Malachy) even against fellow-Vikings to the south of Waterford. The Waterford Vikings succeeded temporarily to the lordship of Dublin after Gluniarainn's death but in 994 Mael Sechlainn drove them out, taking as part of his booty the sacred pagan treasure known as Thor's ring and also a ceremonial sword, 'Charles's sword', that possibly because of some association with Charlemagne or one of the later Carolingians had been taken to be a symbol of the power of the Dublin Vikings. In Dublin itself another of Olaf Cuaran's sons, Sihtric of the Silken Beard succeeded to the kingship. Sihtric's kingship was closely bound up with the career of the greatest hero in early Irish history, that of Brian Boru. Born in 941 in the eastern half of the modern county of Clare, Brian won his early reputation in ceaseless warfare against the Scandinavian settlers. At the age of 26 he won a great victory against the Danes of Limerick, expelling the king Ivor, and sacking the town and port completely. Ivor returned two years later, but in 977, partly in vengeance of the murder of his brother, Mahon, Brian again devastated the settlement, killing Ivor and two of his sons. Brian further completed his revenge in the following year when he killed a third of Ivor's sons and became universally recognised as king of Cashel. By 984 he had extended his overlordship over southern Ireland and for the following 15 years established a somewhat uneasy balance of power with the northern Irish under Mael Sechlainn. Complicated alliances among the petty princes caused a break in the balance. Revolts against Brian's overlordship precipitated war, and in 999 after a particularly ferocious battle Brian captured Dublin. Sihtric came to terms, submitted to Brian who recognised the territorial integrity of Dublin provided that the Danes agreed to fight for him. Mael Seachlinn, who appears as a man of considerable statesmanship, also came to terms, yielding the superiority of his high-kingship to Brian in 1001–2. Other kings of the north made their peace. In 1005 at Armagh Brian was being styled *imperator Scottorum*, emperor of the Irish.

Brian's high-kingship lasted ten years and left legends more potent in Irish history than the reality it embodied. Dissensions among the Irish rulers broke out into the open in 1012 and the political tensions were resolved in one of the great battles of Northern and Western history, the battle of Clontarf, fought on Good Friday, 23 April 1014, shortly after the death of Sweyn Forkbeard in the moment of his triumph in England in the February of that year. The battle was not a straight issue between Irish and Vikings; a strong detachment of Vikings from the Isle of Man supported Brian Boru and the Irish themselves were far from united in their allegiance. Nor was it a straight issue between the forces of centralisation represented by Brian and the forces of localism and disruption. The tendency now indeed is to emphasise the importance of Clontarf as part of the internal Irish struggle for sovereignty, essentially as 'the revolt of the Leinstermen against the dominance of Brian, a revolt in which their Norse allies played an important but secondary role'.[5] There were probably too many swirling crosscurrents of personal ambition and chance encounter for any single issue to stand out. There were Christians on both sides and pagans on both sides. Sihtric of the Silken Beard, lord of Dublin, played a curious and untypical obscure part in the battle, though his position in Dublin was one of the key factors in the campaign. Brian Boru himself remained aloof, intervening only indecisively in the early stages of the quarrel and withdrawing to pray (it was Good Friday and the devout Brian would not fight) in the course of the battle itself. Sihtric had personally enlisted help along the whole length and breadth of the Western Viking world. Sigurd the Stout, the earl of Orkney, Brodir from the Isle of Man (with twenty ships), and Vikings from as far afield as Iceland and Normandy had gathered in a great fleet in the spring of 1014, ostensibly to support their fellow Scandinavians in the fortified market of Dublin. Men's motives, described at great length in later saga accounts, were as diverse as might be expected, a compound of avarice, ambition and honourable desire to support recognised kinsfolk. The result was in a sense a victory and a loss to both sides.

3. Ireland and the Irish Sea, from Gwyn Jones *A History of the Vikings.*

Brian, his son and his grandson were all killed in the battle or its aftermath. On the Viking side Sigurd and Brodir both perished. Brian in legend was held to have saved Ireland by his victory, but it is hard to say from what. None of the Vikings aspired to his high-kingship. The Scandinavian settlements were too useful to the native Irish to be eradicated, but they were not strong or numerous enough to aspire to complete political mastery. In the event the dynastic turbulence that followed Clontarf led to a weakening of Brian's moves towards unity, and the Scandinavian settlements remained, though that degree more strongly confined. Mael Seachlinn was once again recognised as high king but Scandinavian kings continued to exercise authority at Dublin (Sihtric of the Silken Beard himself survived there until the 1030s) and in their fortified markets while a heavily Scandinavianised population continued to flourish at Waterford, Wexford, Cork and to some extent Limerick. In 1052 a disastrous defeat led to the flight of the Scandinavian king from Dublin, but the old dynasty returned again in the early twelfth century and not until the 1160s were the Scandinavian princelings finally removed as part of the complicated process that brought the Anglo-Normans into Ireland. Even then the integrity and special nature of the settlements continued to be recognised by the existence of the so-called Ostmen, often retaining their Scandinavian names and institutions, who continued to play an important role in the trade of the western seaboard from their established centre at Dublin and the other four cities of the Irish-Scandinavian trading world: Waterford, Wexford, Cork and Limerick.

Scotland, the Northern Isles, the Western Isles, and Man

No part of Great Britain was more directly affected by the Scandinavian invasions than the elaborate complex of islands that stretches from the tip of Shetland south-west around the coast of Scotland into the Irish Sea, islands that we know as the Shetlands, the Orkneys, the Hebrides, the Sudreys, and Man – or sometimes in simpler but more archaic fashion as the Nordreys and the Sudreys. We have seen already how many of these islands were early settled by Norwegians. They remained on one of the main Viking routes, subject to raids and settlement sporadically throughout the Viking Age. They were also vastly important staging posts for many enterprises further south, a useful intermediary point for raiding fleets from Scandinavia, convenient places to refit and to recover from the arduous sea passage from Nidaros, the western fjords, or the Vik. In 1066 Orkney played a big part in the events that led up to the battles of Fulford Gate and Stamford Bridge, and it was to Orkney that the young prince Olaf Haroldsson brought the pitiful remnant of the Scandinavian host after the defeat at Stamford Bridge.

And yet, perhaps because of the very mobility of the Scandinavians, there is no part of Great Britain where political history is more obscure. There is plentiful vigorous saga material, notably that preserved in the Orkneyinga Saga, but it is difficult to do more than show the bare outline of the political history of the islands. The clearest glimpses come when Norwegian kings such as Harold Fairhair in the 9th century or Magnus Barefoot at the end of the eleventh decide to assert Norwegian overlordship and to suppress piracy or incipient revolt from nests of exiles and renegades who had found island refuges to their taste. Otherwise it is often a matter of piecing together fragments of information about ambitious chieftains, Irish and Scottish, as well as the dominant Norse, who from time to time assert their authority over part or whole of the complex of islands.

The most important and most prosperous of the settlements – with the possible exception of Man – was the settlement in Orkney. The family of Ragnald, jarl of Möre in western Norway, which provided Normandy with its ducal house, was also prominent in Orkney affairs. Ragnald's brother, Sigurd the Great, had acted more or less as Harold Fairhair's regent and had won control of extensive territory in north Scotland in Caithness, Sutherland, and even into Ross-shire and south of the Moray Firth. Ragnald's youngest son, Turf-Einar, did not enjoy the same extensive authority as his uncle Sigurd, but later poetic and part legendary accounts attributed to him not only the credit for introducing the skills of the peat-burner to the islanders but also the credit for setting up the earl's authority and power on a more territorial basis. He was reputed to have paid a substantial fine on behalf of the islanders (60 marks of gold) to the Norwegian king in return for the surrender on the part of the free farmers of their odal rights to him. The story has the smack of the later twelfth- or thirteenth-century feudal world to it, but there may be some truth in the idea that the family of Ragnald was trying to consolidate its position in Orkney at least during the early part of the tenth century.[6] The middle years of the tenth century saw no dramatic watershed in events of the type we have seen in Scandinavian affairs elsewhere in Britain. As far as there is one single dominant thread to the political story it concerns the fortunes of the house of Ragnald, its marriage alliances, its quarrels with other powers (including fellow-Vikings such as the dynasty of Limerick Vikings established in Man) and its relationship – which generally followed the theme of nominal dependence and virtual independence – with the Norwegian crown. Caithness was brought back into the Orkney orbit by a marriage agreement made by one of Turf-Einar's sons and a princess of the mainland. Further dynastic marriages with Irish chieftains brought extra influence and security in the Western Isles. The son of one of these marriages, Sigurd the Stout, brought fresh prestige to the dynasty at the end of the tenth and the beginning of the eleventh century. Christianity was certainly not unknown in the islands at an earlier date, but in 995 Sigurd suffered a conversion as sudden and dramatic if not as deep and long-lasting as any in recorded history. We are told that the stormy, newly-converted Olaf Tryggvasson came across him suddenly and by chance in the bay of Osmondwall (Kirk Hope) and gave him the straight choice of death and destruction or conversion.[7] The dramatic nature of this account, taken from the Orkneyinga Saga, must not obscure the fact that many men in the Northern Isles were Christians long before 995. Sigurd accepted conversion, built up a powerful hold on Caithness and the Southern Isles, placed a subordinate earl in charge of Man, and married as his second wife a daughter of Malcolm II of Scotland (1005–34). He was the lynch-pin of the Viking federation hastily summoned to the aid of the Dublin Vikings in 1014 and his death at the resulting battle of Clontarf was as momentous in Northern history as the death of Brian Boru himself. He was succeeded by his son, Thorfinn later known as 'the Mighty', the most colourful of the Orkney earls (1014–64). Thorfinn's inheritance was turbulent. For the first 20 years of his active political life up to the death of his grandfather, Malcolm of Scotland, he was engaged in family feuding with his half-brothers and power-sharing in the islands (under the watchful eye in the 1020s of Olaf Haraldsson, St Olaf of Norway). Malcolm's death was followed by an unsuccessful attempt on the part of his successor, Duncan I (1034–40) to recover Caithness, an attempt which left Thorfinn temporarily confirmed in the leadership of all the Northern Vikings. Norwegian interference at the time of Magnus Olafsson forced further power-sharing in the Orkneys, this time with Ragnald, the son of Thorfinn's half-brother, Brusi. The arrangement worked well until the mid-1040s when a violent quarrel sprang up that ended with the slaying of Ragnald as he fled from his blazing Orkney homestead at Christmas-tide. For the greater part of the reign of Edward the Confessor in England (1042–66) and of Harold Hardrada in Norway (1047–66) Thorfinn consolidated his hold on the northern and western seaways of Britain. He was a Christian and founded the first regular bishop's see in the Northern Isles at Birsay where he was given Christian burial at his death in 1064. He was strong enough and confident enough to journey abroad and record has survived of a visit to Rome, as well as of visits to Denmark and to German imperial lands. He recognised the overlordship of Hardrada, king of Norway, while enjoying almost unfettered rule of Shetland, Orkney and the Hebrides. He also governed the Sudreys and (after 1034) reasserted the rights of the Orkney earls over Man. His relationship with the Scottish kings was predictably complex. At the height of his power Thorfinn was said to have held no fewer than nine Scottish earldoms, including Ross, a part of Moray, and Galloway. It is hard to know how much to make of this. He was certainly effective in the northern mainland and also in Galloway where he liked to reside and which he liked to use as a base for ventures in the Southern Isles and Man. Towards the end of his life the formidable new Scottish king, Malcolm Canmore, Malcolm III (1058–93), asserted his rights over most of mainland Scotland. Thorfinn's achievements were beyond question great, but it would be utterly wrong to consider him as a builder of a permanent empire of the Isles and of Man. His authority depended much on his personal vigour and on his personal presence. His father Sigurd is said to have granted back odal rights to the Orkney landowners and whatever truth there may or may not be in that precise statement it is beyond question that the basic social composition on most of the islands consisted of hardy independent fishermen-farmers, only too ready to turn to Viking enterprise if the leadership were good and the prospects for profit reasonable. Thorfinn's basic achievement was to sharpen for these men their sense of awareness of common kinship with the Norwegian homeland, not to mould them into a permanent independent polity. By the time of his death or very soon after the Isle of Man passed under the control of Vikings from Dublin. Godfred Sihtricson, one of the survivors from Stamford Bridge, is described as a king of Man. He took back with him from Stamford Bridge Godred Crovan, a man whose father was an Icelander, and Godred after a chequered career in Norway itself won a kingship in Man for himself (1079–95), transmitting rights to his descendants notably to his son Olaf who governed Man from 1113 to 1153. Orkney itself tended to be divided and subdivided amongst the numerous heirs of Thorfinn after 1064 – a ready and natural fate for any island polity – until the Norwegian king Magnus Barefoot intervened in person towards the end of the eleventh century. We have already seen the disastrous impact of his activities on Welsh affairs in 1098. In the Orkneys he removed the quarrelsome earls and put his own son Sigurd in command. Further south he saw to it – probably the main object of his expedition – that the Sudreys and Man paid their tribute to their rightful king, the ruler of Norway. After Sigurd himself became the Norwegian king in 1103, the grandsons of Thorfinn were permitted to resume earlish office in the North. Northern Island history remained turbulent and fluctuating throughout the twelfth and most of the thirteenth century, but we now move out of the true Viking Age. Man and the Western Isles remained under nominal and at times effective Norwegian overlordship until 1266, when after a series of Scottish victories the young king Magnus ceded to Alexander II of Scotland the lordship of the Isle of Man and of all the Sudreys in return for a payment of 4,000 marks (at the rate of 1,000 marks a year) and of 100 marks a year thereafter. Orkney and Shetland were under Scandinavian sovereignty for a further two centuries. The earls became Scottish, and Norway itself became part of a joint kingdom of Denmark–Norway, ruled by a Danish dynasty. The 100 marks a year payment, agreed on in 1266, was paid only intermittently, and in the 1460s the final attempt at a solution to the problem of the islands was in fact made. In 1468 a marriage contract was arranged between King James III of Scotland and Margaret, a Danish princess, the daughter of King Christian I. The agreement was drawn up formally on 8 September. Christian remitted the annual payment of 100 marks, forgave all the accumulated arrears, and granted 60,000 Rhenish florins as his daughter's dowry, 10,000 to be paid in cash and the other 50,000 promised with the Orkneys held in pledge until the debt was redeemed. Christian could not find even the 10,000 initial payment, and so on 28 May 1469, he pledged Shetland on the same conditions for 8,000 of the promised florins. The islands were pawned not ceded, but political circumstances ensured that the arrangements should become permanent. Shetland came in almost fortuitously: earlier efforts to link it with the Faroes had not proved successful. On the same day as he pawned Shetland King Christian I wrote to the inhabitants of Orkney and Shetland, instructing them to do homage to the Scottish king and to pay their taxes to him until the islands were redeemed. More than half a millennium later they are still doing so: an odd quirk of an end to a brave story of colonisation and settlement from the Viking Age.[8]

7.

The Effects of the Scandinavian Invasions on Britain : The Problem of Settlement

To this point we have been concerned mainly with the general political impact of the Scandinavian invasions on Britain. The time has now come to attempt a deeper evaluation of the effects. It is well realised, of course, that some of these effects, some indeed of the most important of them, are beyond the province of the historian, given our present limitations of admissible evidence. The sheer addition in genetic terms of Scandinavian blood into the human stock peopling these islands must have been considerable. Inter-marriage was never discouraged and a recognised place was found in Scandinavian legal systems for sexual unions that fell well short of recognisable Christian marriage. Study of blood groups and methods of evaluation of nigrescence are imperfect disciplines and with each generation that passes hope of establishing regional variations that will help to trace direct Scandinavian influence from the time of the migration grows dimmer and dimmer. And yet historians are right still to think in these human terms. Over large tracts of the British Isles the Scandinavians formed an important recognisable element in the human population. The Middle Ages was fully aware of this, and treated the matter as a commonplace. When Giraldus Cam-brensis wished to explain the origins of the peculiar style of part-singing characteristic of Wales and of the lands beyond the Humber and on the borders of Yorkshire, he attributed it directly to the Danes and Norwegians by whom those parts of the island were frequently ruled. It is a pleasant thought that to one shrewd medieval observer characteristics common to the ancestors of the Treorchy Male Voice Choir and the choral societies of Leeds and Huddersfield were attributable to a common subjection to Scandinavian mastery.[1]

The main source of evidence for adequate discussion of intensity of settlement are relatively prosaic, and all have limitations and imperfections. The existence of distinctive art forms, classified in orderly though at times overlapping chronological sequence help to indicate strong Scandinavian presence in Britain. The Borre and Jellinge styles of the first Viking Age lead into the Mammen, Ringerike and Urnes style of the later tenth and eleventh centuries. Stone crossses and memorial slabs provide the most fruitful, truly monumental, sources, but the interlace, and the main zoomorphic elements in birds and beasts, are to be found also on small metal-work objects and fragments of carved wood. Examples are widespread throughout Scandinavian Britain, in the Vale of Pickering in east Yorkshire, in the north-west, and most powerfully in the Isle of Man itself. Current orthodox opinion would attribute native stylistic forms, even the Anglian characteristics of the Middleton sculptures and Irish elements in the Isle of Man, to something of a secondary nature. The vital creative stylistic impulses seem to have been generated in Scandinavian soil, though modifications particularly where a strong native tradition of stone-carving is known to have flourished, at times lead the archaeologist or art historian inevitably to talk in the rather awkward terms of 'insular-Jellinge' or 'insular-Ringerike'. The force of the artistic impulse extended well beyond the Danelaw in space and beyond the Norman Conquest in time. One of the finest examples of modified Ringerike occurs in the early eleventh-century tombstone found in St Paul's churchyard, London. The vigorous and imaginative school of stone sculpture centred at Kilpeck in Herefordshire in mid-twelfth century bore the characteristics of developed Urnes style. However intimate the intermingling of Celtic, Anglian and Viking elements the lesson of the art historian teaches us not to underestimate the direct and enduring influence of Scandinavia on British life.

The principal and strongest body of evidence relating to Scandinavian settlement comes, however, from language sources, among which place-name and personal name evidence take on a special life of their own, and from evidence drawn from institutional sources. In language matters England is in a separate and distinctive category within the British scene. Anglo-Saxon was a Germanic language, cognate to and in basic structure very similar to Old Norse. An Icelandic author could comment in the thirteenth century that up to the time of William the Bastard the language of England was one and the same as that in Norway and Denmark, and that it was only after his conquest that there was a change of tongue to French – because William was of French extraction.[2] The conventions of writing tend to exaggerate rather than diminish the differences between the two Germanic languages for the simple reason that the Old Norse written sources are so much later in date than the Anglo-Saxon, but enough of the similarities shine through in any comparison of similar passages, especially those of scriptural material, in Old English, and Old Norse. There was more to it than mere regional dialectical variation, but missionaries, traders and soldiers seem to have experienced very little linguistic difficulty in moving from England to the Scandinavian North. This is a point, of course, of marked contrast with the rest of the British Isles. The Celtic tongues, Goidelic or Brythonic, of Ireland, Scotland and Wales, were Indo-European, but remote in structure, sound-change, and vocabulary from the Germanic tongues. Conscious and sustained effort had to be made by Celtic-speakers and Scandinavians alike in order to understand and be understood. There could be no slow folding together of language elements such as occurred in the Danelaw in England. Linguistic evidence therefore demands a different and in some respects a more cautious approach in relation to English problems than in relation to the Celtic world. By 1100 the very nature of the English language itself in the east and north had been profoundly modified to the point where it is not unreasonable to call it Anglo-Scandinavian; and it was from the language pattern of eastern England that the main lines of standard modern English were ultimately to develop.

The whole linguistic situation in England is complicated by the poverty of written record in Old Norse that can be ascribed to the period of invasion and settlement. There is no surviving substantial literary text, and the assumption is that when the Scandinavian settlers were converted to Christianity, the religion of written record, they were also converted linguistically to the use of Latin and of Anglo-Saxon. Archbishop Wulfstan was bishop of Worcester and archbishop of York from 1002 to 1023. He was a conscientious bishop and a voluminous and effective writer and teacher. The Scandinavian element in his vocabulary was distinctly large and gives a quite individual character to many of his homilies as well as to his legal writings. His language is nevertheless unmistakably Anglo-Saxon, and indeed basically the language of Wessex, the accepted *Schriftssprache* of late Anglo-Saxon England.[3] Attempts to prove Anglian peculiarities as opposed to West Saxon have not been successful. If this is true of Wulfstan whose archiepiscopal diocese contained the heavily Scandinavian centre of York and whose king was finally Cnut, how much more true it is of other late Old English writers. There is no fragment of the Gospels, no scriptural text, no liturgical phrase which can be traced to an Old Norse speaker resident in England. The converted Dane worshipped in English – or in Latin. Orm, the son of Gamol, renewed the church of St Gregory in heavily Scandinavianised Kirkdale in Yorkshire in the days of Earl Tostig (1055–65). He recorded his munificence in a still surviving inscription attached to the sundial over the lintel of the south porch and the language used in the inscription was standard Old English with Northumbrian features and only one obvious Scandinavian loanword (*solmerca* (sun-marking) from the Old Norse *solmerki*).[4] When a writ was issued in the middle years of the eleventh century by Gospatric, lord of Allerdale and Dalston, relating to grants of lands and rights in Cumberland, the language used was Old English in spite of the fact that the principal men concerned bore Scandinavian names; indeed the use of the Old Norse term *dreng* in the writ may be taken as evidence that drengs were as firmly naturalised in the social scene of northern England as were earls throughout the length and breadth of the country.[5]

The Scandinavians were not however completely illiterate. There are a number of runic inscriptions in England, many of which for simple natural reasons of weathering have been worn away to the point where they are virtually illegible. Inscriptions on sword-hilts, bone combs, as well as on funerary stones show that Old Norse remained a fully inflected language, subject to the same sound changes and developments in England as back home in the Scandinavian mainland. The phrases inscribed are naturally standard and often not particularly informative: 'Thorfastr made a good comb' (on a bone comb found at Lincoln); 'Ginna and Toki had this stone set up' (on a stone in St Paul's churchyard, London); 'Dolfinn wrote these runes on this stone' (graffito within the cathedral at Carlisle). The custom of fashioning runic inscriptions persisted long and there are occasionally more interesting examples to be found in the twelfth or even the thirteenth century. Towards the end of the eleventh or the beginning of the twelfth century Mael-Lomchon, a Manx Norseman (together with the daughter of Dubh-Gael whom Aðils had to wife) raised a cross in memory of her foster-mother, Mael-Muire, adding a gnomic comment 'it is better to leave a good foster-son than a bad son'. A full runic inscription from mid-twelfth century at Maeshowe in Orkney tells how:

> The crusaders to Jerusalem broke open the Orkney grave-mound. In the north-west is the great treasure hidden, which was left behind (after death); great treasure was hidden. Happy is he who can find this great wealth.
>
> Those runes that man cut who is most skilled in runecraft, west over sea, with that axe which Gauk, Trandil's son, in the south (of Iceland) owned.

The skill of carving runes persisted, notably in the ambiance of Man, Ireland and the islands. On the Scandinavian/Irish mainland of north-west England as late as the mid-twelfth century an inscription was cut in runes on the tympanum of the old church at Pennington in Furness that appears to record that 'Gamal founded [*seti?*] this church; Hubert the mason carved [it?]'. The latest interpreter of this badly weathered Pennington inscription, after pointing to the difficulties of obtaining an accurate reading, rightly concludes that one of the big lessons to be learnt from it is that the two languages remained in intimate contact in north-west England in the twelfth century.[6]

Old Norse continued therefore to be spoken in Britain well beyond the Viking period. Even after proper discount is made for the conservative nature of those who carve runes, it is clear that British Old Norse was exceedingly tenacious of old forms, to the point indeed where it must have appeared archaic to the rest of the Scandinavian world. Under the powerful influence of early Middle English it became corrupt and anglicised even in the north-west, though the strong element of Scandinavian language forms in the great alliterative verse of the north-west in the fourteenth century testifies to its tenacity. There appears to have been very little difference between east and west Scandinavian, between Danish and Norwegian, at the time of the settlement, though it is possible, partly by peculiarities of vocabulary structure to distinguish between word borrowings that are specifically Danish and those that are specifically Norwegian, for example words that assimilate *ht*, *nk*, or *nt*, and are borrowed in assimilated form into Middle English betray probable Norwegian origin – *stutte* (to stint), *rukke* (wrinkle), *slakke* (hollow); words that are unquestionably Danish include *tro* (faith), *lune* (peace) and *boþ* (both).

Enough has been said to show that Old Norse was spoken and understood in England after the end of the Viking Age. It is likely that it remained more or less intelligible in the Danelaw at least into the first or second generation after the Norman Conquest and that traders at York (and indeed in London) found little language difficulty until about the mid-twelfth century. In the main Anglo-Saxon and its successor early Middle English triumphed as the current everyday language. Officially, too, at the local level English proved overwhelmingly strong. Communications by sea remained important, and contacts with the Isle of Man, the Irish ports and the Northern and Western Isles, all of which contained a substantial and influential Norse-speaking population well into the twelfth century (and in some instances much later), helped to keep the

Norse tongue alive. Traditional literary Anglo-Saxon, affected by the conservatism of a mature written convention, shows (except in the legal field) comparatively little sign of this long linguistic symbiosis. The spoken language, especially in the north and east, was a very different matter. The impact of Old Norse on English vocabulary was deep and widespread. The process of borrowing and of assimilation appears to have been continuous throughout the Viking period and into the twelfth century. Few Norse loanwords, if any, were borrowed from the Continent after about the middle of the tenth century. Borrowings are more intimate, arising from communities dwelling closely together, intermingling and inter-marrying, subjects of the same Christian kings, English or Danish or Norman. The vocabulary so acquired enriched English not in an exotic, specialised sense but in a most general sense. Words to denote the most common of actions ('to call' and 'to take') were adopted. Household, everyday words such as 'husband', 'window', 'knife', 'fellow' were absorbed into what must truly be called an Anglo-Scandinavian Germanic language. Even the inner core of the language, pronoun structure and terms connected with the family, were affected. The pronoun structure of Anglo-Saxon had developed along lines that must have led to serious ambiguities in the spoken tongue, notably in relation to the third person plural. Borrowings from Scandinavian sources (though there are some indications notably in the Sherborne Cartulary of indigenous moves in this direction) helped to clarify the situation, and 'they', 'them', 'their' became part of the basic structure of the language. Other words essential to the grammatical flexibility of the language were also introduced or modified by contact with Old Norse. Modern English 'sister' owes its final form more to Old Norse *syster* than to Old English *sweoster*. Even the word 'to die' is probably derived from the West Norse *deyja* (an unrecorded Old English *dēgan* is possible, but it is at least odd that such a basic word should not be recorded in the extensive Old English literature). In more specialised fields, notably the fields of law and administration, Old Norse influence is heavy ('law', itself, 'outlaw', 'earl' in the new administrative eleventh-century sense in place of Old English *ealdorman*, 'hold', 'husting' to describe the regular weekly court for the settlement of civil business in pre-Conquest London, 'thrall', and a whole mass of precise legal terminology such as *grith* (peace) in its various forms). The language evidence remains the cornerstone of the argument in favour of an interpretation of the Scandinavian invasion and settlement of England that will stress the numbers, influence and permanent effects of the Scandinavian newcomers.[7]

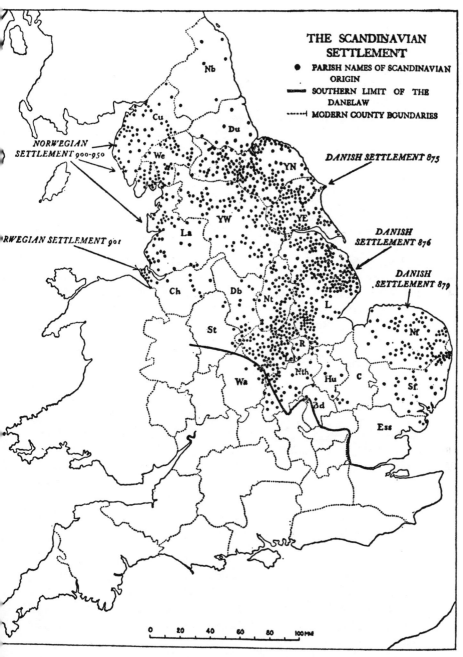

THE SCANDINAVIAN
SETTLEMENT

● PARISH NAMES OF SCANDINAVIAN
ORIGIN

━━ SOUTHERN LIMIT OF THE
DANELAW

----┤ MODERN COUNTY BOUNDARIES

*NORWEGIAN
SETTLEMENT 900-950*

DANISH SETTLEMENT 875

NORWEGIAN SETTLEMENT 901

*DANISH
SETTLEMENT 876*

*DANISH
SETTLEMENT 879*

Nb
Cu
Du
We
YN
YW
YE
La
Ch
Db
Nt
L
Nf
St
R
Le
Wa
Nth
Hu
C
Sf
Bd
Ess

0   20   40   60   80   100 MM

4. Scandinavian settlement in Britain, from Gwyn Jones *A History of the Vikings*.

The most fruitful and in many respects the best-known source of ancillary evidence for an investigation of Scandinavian settlement in depth is the evidence of place-names, in itself a somewhat special and precise branch of language study. A cursory glance at the map of the parish names of England is enough to show a dramatic difference between the north and the east, 'Danish England', on the one hand, and the south and west, 'English England' on the other. North and east of the political line of demarcation established by Alfred and Guthrum in the ninth century (Watling Street and the river Lea) Scandinavian names proliferate and occasionally dominate; south and east, apart from a slight trickle into Warwickshire and Northamptonshire, they scarcely exist. Field names and minor names of all types, especially the names of streams and small rivers, reveal the speech habits of the settlers themselves, and they further reinforce firmly the simple conclusion that can be drawn from the first cursory glance. In half of England the basic settlement names were heavily modified by Scandinavian influence; the other half was virtually untouched. Within 'Danish' England itself of course the pattern, even at the superficial level, was far from uniform. In the extreme north-east (Northumberland and Durham) and the south-east (Essex and Hertfordshire) Danish names are few and scarce. The north-west, as we have already seen, may more properly be called Norwegian than Danish, fading into a Danish area in south Lancashire to a border-county of Staffordshire where again Scandinavian names are few and concentrated mostly on the east. East Anglia, as always, is a special case with plentiful though at times ambiguous evidence of the Danish presence. Heavy concentration of Danish place-names occur in two principal areas, the territory of the Five Boroughs, and the lands dependent on the army settled at York. Over a long tract of country stretching from the mouth of the Humber through Lindsey, Nottinghamshire and Leicestershire, Danish names are thick on the ground, giving trace of the settlement achieved by armies and their followers based on the Five Boroughs of Lincoln, Stamford, Nottingham, Leicester, and to a lesser extent Derby. In the Ridings of Yorkshire (and the term 'riding' itself is Scandinavian in origin) Danish names are plentiful, notably in parts of the North and East Riding. The West Riding has not such a concentration of Danish names, except in the lower Don and around York, while Norwegian elements are powerful in Nidderdale, Calderdale and Craven. The fact of Scandinavian presence is unavoidable: the only questions that remain concern its density and intensity.

The most interesting and revealing onomastic elements are names containing the Scandinavian elements -by and -thorpe, those containing the Old English element -tun, together with a Scandinavian first element, and those representing replacements or substitutions of accredited Old English names by Scandinavian (Whitby for *Streoneshalh* and Derby for *Northworthige* are perhaps the best known of these). Modern work on these elements has enriched our knowledge by refusing to treat them merely as linguistic phenomena and by relating them firmly to the geographical, topographical and even geological reality they were meant to represent.[8] For example, it is now generally accepted that the numerous elements in -by represent for the most part (not completely since -by remained an acceptable naming form even after the Norman Conquest) settlements established by the Danes in the first full flood of their migration in the generations after the success of their armies in the 860s and 870s. In the areas of the Five Boroughs and in Yorkshire they often represent the colonisation of the best available land. Once political mastery was recognised indeed the Scandinavian settlement was in many areas juxtaposed to not superimposed upon the existing English villages, hamlets and farms. There was plenty of land available. In Leicestershire the main Danish settlement was made not so much in the already thickly populated valley of the Soar but in the valley of the Wreak and its tributaries. The very name of the river was changed from what was probably its English name of Eye (still used of the upper reaches) to the Danish 'Wreak', meaning 'the winding one'. Similar evidence for the setting up of colonising groups of -bys behind the protecting hand of the armies may be discerned in Nottinghamshire and Derbyshire. These settlers could well have come along the traditional migrant route of Humber, Trent, and its tributaries with little direct impetus from the army headquarters at Nottingham, or Derby. A very heavy concentration of -bys is to be found in the Lincolnshire Wolds, and again the most intelligible explanation, borne out by dialectic study and examination of field-names is that this indicates a steady successful and early migration through the natural route of Grimsby and the mouth of the Humber. The Yorkshire evidence, taken too in conjunction with reasonable inference from dialectical and personal name customs, seems finally conclusive. The -bys, so many of which are compounded with a Danish personal name, often of an early type, are based in large part on successful colonising ventures which were probably initiated in the last quarter of the 9th century or the early years of the tenth.

Names in -thorpe present special difficulties, so much so that some leading scholars have at times rejected them as sound evidence for early colonising phases. They are however (like the -bys) pre-dominantly compounded with Scandinavian elements and their number and topographical distribution speak strongly in favour of an interpretation which would see in them evidence of secondary settlement at an early stage. In Yorkshire, in particular, the name-form was often associated with settlements that concentrated on sheep-farming. The territory of the Five Boroughs presents a more complicated picture, but there again -thorpe is used of a secondary settlement, hamlet or farmstead, a dependency of a larger settlement and probably representing a later stratum in the name-giving process than the more numerous -bys. Leicestershire and Lincoln-shire stand out as counties rich in -thorpes and heavily settled by Danish colonists.

To concentrate merely on the -bys and -thorpes, however, gives a somewhat misleading picture. They contain a high proportion of new settlements, good evidence indeed for a colonising move, but far from the whole story. The Danes did not enter an empty land, nor did they clear the land of indigenous inhabitants before turning to settlement themselves. Theirs was a settlement on terms, buttressed by military power but not accompanied by wholesale massacre and eviction. Place-names survive in pure unadulterated English forms even in the most heavily Danicised areas. There also exists a sub-stantial body of names in the Danelaw proper that contain a first element in a Danish personal name, compounded with the English element -tun (a village in a farmstead). These names are known, not completely happily but conveniently, as 'Grimston hybrids'. They have to be handled with care, but many of them represent English villages taken over and renamed by the Danes. Local circumstances determined whether -tun or -by was used in some instances, but again in general Grimston names are common in districts where there is a preponderance of English names and very few -by names. The quality of agricultural land on which the Grimstons are to be found is consistently good; the Danish names are often early or rare or both; they are more common in the westerly parts of the Danelaw (Nottinghamshire and Leicestershire) than in the east; and they may in fact well represent a very early stage in the Danish settlement when army leaders took over the lordship and initiated a degree of settle-ment on already favoured agricultural sites. Much of the most perceptive modern analysis attributes a priority in time to the Grimston hybrids and associates; many of the names may be associated with the earliest stages in Scandinavian settlement, even with the land-taking of the 870s.

Similar intensive work to that already done on the place-names of the Five Boroughs and of Yorkshire has not yet been done – and may indeed never be possible – on other areas of 'Danish England'. In the north-west inversion compounds such as Aspatria (that is to say names consisting of a noun followed by an adjectival element (Patrick's ash tree in this instance) in Celtic order rather than normal Germanic order with preceding adjective) betray the presence of Scandinavians who have dwelt for generations among a Celtic-speaking people, residents of the Isle of Man or the Scottish Isles or Ireland, generally termed Irish/Norwegians. Other names are of pure Norwegian type and appear to have been given by colonists who moved in rapidly to these western Northumbrian lands, perhaps using the Scottish islands as mere staging posts on their journey south. The place-name structure of Cumbria, and of Cumberland in particular, however, gives an intelligible picture of early English penetration of the lowland and coastal fringe valleys where there was good arable, with the mountain heart still sub-stantially in British hands. In the fells and dales of Cumberland and to a lesser extent Westmorland and parts of Lancashire British displacement where it occurs at all seems to have been at the hands of Scandinavian rather than Anglo-Saxon settlers. Recent exact work on ancillary language evidence concerning especially botanical terms substantiates the view that the special gifts of the Irish/ Norwegians lay in the fields of pastoral economy, and that their shielings were newly established in the early tenth century in the upland areas where the good soil shades off into adequate or hard pasture and rock. Norwegian penetration followed the natural routes into the Pennines and the West Riding of Yorkshire: field names and dialectic forms in Dentdale in particular indicate strong Norwegian presence.[9] As we have already seen the existence of an Irish-Norwegian kingdom at York until 954 A.D. makes such pene-tration fully intelligible, but again one must seek to oversimplify what was a very complicated human process of movement and settlement. Inversion compounds in Yorkshire itself have turned out to be largely illusory, and it is clearly unscholarly to profess a too certain classification of names into neat categories of Dane and Norwegian. North of the Tees, in spite of the attraction of the country around Tyneside and north to the fluctuating Scottish border there was comparatively little Scandinavian settlement, although the Danelaw in theory at least extended to the Tyne. Durham (O.E. *dun*, a hill, and Scandinavian *holm*, an island) constitutes an important and possibly somewhat underestimated exception, where there may have been quite strong localised Danish settlement.

As we said at an earlier stage place-name evidence in one sense constitutes no more than a specialised branch of language evidence. The study of personal names is closely associated with it, and as investigation continues into twelfth- and thirteenth-century cartulary and official government records so does the Scandinavian element in the personal name structure of the Danelaw become increasingly apparent. There is a marked contrast again with English England where (with the exception of some boroughs) Scandinavian nomenclature is rare. Modern dialects and even more so the dialects of medieval English constitute another branch – fascinating, at times illuminating, and nearly always treacherous for the wary as well as the unwary. It is probable that great contributions will be made in future from this source towards an understanding of the nature and depth of Scandinavian settlement, but much basic work has to be done on phonology as well as semantics before the dialect material is in full fit state to be absorbed into a historical synthesis. Carefully constructed distribution maps based on the available evidence suggest an approximate line from the Solway Firth to the mouth of the Tees as the northern limit for areas of intensive settlement, while further south the lands around the Humber, north Lindsey and indeed the greater part of Yorkshire seem much more heavily affected by Scandinavian forms than the lands of the southern Danelaw. This could seriously affect our own picture of the Scandinavian settlement, wean us away from Nottingham and Leicester, make us think more energetically of the distortions in our historical record brought about William I's devastation of the North. Other factors, however, provide their own distorting agents to the chief picture. The strength of standard English was greater at an earlier stage for political as well as for geographical and social reasons in Mercia than in Northumbria. A dialectical border roughly from the Ribble to the Humber appeared almost as a dominant feature of the English scene in the Norman and Angevin period. Again one remembers the contrast in solidity of the Norman Conquest and feudal settlement in the land to the south of the Honours of Pontefract, Tickhill and Tutbury with the lands to the north. The tenacity of Norwegian dialect forms, strong even under sophisticated literary forms well into the fourteenth century, is a significant and possibly underestimated feature of the dialectology of parts of the north-west that lie between Ribble and Mersey and spill into the Wirral peninsula. The strength of the overall linguistic evidence, in spite of obvious difficulties of interpretation and of chronology, is great and in potential even greater, but it assumes its maximum importance to the historian only when it is brought into conjunction with the powerful institutional evidence for the presence and influence of the Danes.[10]

Institutional Evidence

Much of the hardest debate of the last generation has been concerned with the density of settlement, the numbers involved, and the chronology. The debate has been hard-fought, good-humoured, and on the whole thoroughly constructive.[11] Linguistic and place-name evidence has properly been at the centre of the debate, but it is also important not to neglect the institutional evidence. By the twelfth century more than a third of the country in areal extent, from the Scottish border to the line drawn by Alfred and Guthrum from Chester along Watling Street to the river Lea and London was known as the Danelaw. Was the description justified and how did the peculiarities manifest themselves?

The Danelaw, of course, as a result of the efforts of the late Old English monarchy was an integral part of the English kingdom. It was divided into shires, some like the massive Yorkshire and Lincolnshire bearing in their extent evidence of the special military and political circumstances that led to their creation. The major subdivisions made necessary by their sheer size were known under the Scandinavian name of trithings (thirds), which gives us our modern familiar 'ridings' of Yorkshire. The Midland shires, dependent on the Danish boroughs of Nottingham, Derby, and Leicester, and the shires of the south-east Danelaw conformed to the normal English pattern. So in all essentials did the great East Anglian divisions of Norfolk and Suffolk. At the time of Domesday Book, again for intelligible political reasons, the north-west was still imperfectly shired but elsewhere at that very important level there was no difference between the Danelaw and the rest of England. Knights of the shire in the thirteenth century and sheriffs were similar creatures whether they hailed from Devon or Derby, Sussex or Suffolk.

Institutionally the further sub-divisions (with the exception of the 'ridings') were also similar though possibly not identical in origin or function. Over most of England, including much of the Danelaw, the principal unit was the hundred, and most of the routine fiscal and disciplinary business of the community passed through the hundred courts. In these parts of England, however, where the Scandinavian presence was the most obvious the equivalent subdivision of a shire was known as a wapentake. The name is interesting, derived as it is through an intermediate Old English form, from the

Old Norse, *vapnatak*, a term used in Scandinavian communities to signify the brandishing of weapons in an assembly to show approval (or possibly of the ceremonial taking up of weapons after an assembly or 'thing' had transacted its business). We find wapentakes in the territory of the Five Boroughs and in the greater part of Yorkshire. It is hard to be certain of significant differences in procedure from the hundred, though we shall discuss some apparent variations in practice that may well have bearing on general legal and indeed constitutional development in the late Saxon and early Norman period. For the moment it is enough to point to the existence of a Scandinavian name for an institution, the wapentake, that must have been the basic legal and constitutional unit for most of the inhabitants of an extensive tract of England.

To be sure the most important single body of evidence relating to the special nature of the Danelaw comes from the legal field. The Danes were a litigious people, and they and the Norwegians also had their own highly developed view of law, of legal right, and of legal institutions and procedures. Chronicles of the twelfth and thirteenth centuries recount how Danish landowners flourished in East Anglia and the Fenlands. A Ramsey writer tells how his abbey acquired lands which Cnut had taken from Englishmen to reward his followers. One estate came as compensation from Thurkill, a Dane, who had perjured himself in court and another was given by Bishop Aethelric who had got the Danish landowner drunk, had taken a wager that he could not raise the purchase price of 50 marks before dawn, and had then galloped to the king (interrupting him at a game of chess) to raise the sum successfully and in good time.[12] These stories bear out other more prosaic records. Easterners were accustomed to the idea of Scandinavian landowners obedient in their violent way to the law. There remained, however, in England something of a contradiction and a paradox. Important modifications were made to legal practice and vocabulary; and yet the laws of Cnut which served as a model of legal utterance for the succeeding century were in the full stream of English legal achievement, in natural line of succession from the legislative activity of Edgar the Peaceful. There was, as far as one can judge, nothing approaching the juridicial revolution which accompanied the Norwegian settlement of the Northern Isles and of Man.

There are perfectly intelligible reasons for this difference. Danish institutions were close to the Anglo-Saxon. Both communities had long traditions of kindred organisation, wergeld payments, and of public assemblies. The only major difference lay in the field of religion, and as the Danes were converted so did the closeness of institutional life tend to become yet more intimate. Acceptance of the Christian Church involved acceptance of a considerable mass of Anglo-Saxon law and custom. It also involved acceptance of a body of men – the clergy – who were the chief instruments for the written recording of law. Indeed it is possible that oral custom in the northern things and wapentakes of the Danelaw differed more than the written record will ever permit us to appreciate. Similarities in social structure and legal habit explain basic assimilation better than any attempted distinction between proud, excessively legalistic Norwegian and more complacent Dane.

From the written record itself enough has survived to point to the Danish contribution. Edgar in one of his codes expressly permitted (in 962–3) the Danes to exercise their secular rights 'according to the good laws they can best decide on'.[13] Safeguards against theft, notably the provision of good witness (in wapentakes as well as in hundreds and boroughs) were to apply to all the nation, whether Englishmen, Danes, or Britons, but the special mention of secular right among the Danes nevertheless has great constitutional force and interest. Ethelred, in an early statement of law which he made at Wantage deep in the heart of historic Wessex, found it helpful to issue a code for the men of the Five Boroughs more or less side by side with a corresponding code 'according to the law of the English'.[14] Private compilations in the late Anglo-Saxon period dealt with the Law of the Northumbrian People and also outlined in an elaborate detail which betrayed fear of heathenism the 'Law of the Northumbrian Priests'.[15] Permanent basic differences may not have been effected, but the day-to-day legal practice in much of England for the greater part of the tenth and eleventh centuries was surely distinctive enough fully to merit the descriptive term the 'Danelaw' which contemporaries ascribed to it.

Some of these practices coincided well enough with Anglo-Saxon customs to be generally acceptable. It must be remembered that no thoroughgoing contemporary discussion of legal procedure such as we have from the age of Glanville or even more so Bracton, was ever made in Anglo-Saxon England. We have to rely on occasional references in law codes or charters or other diplomatic documents. Terminology in relation to land transactions suggests heavy Scandinavian influence, and it is especially interesting to note that a typical system of reliance on independent sureties (*festermen*) was invoked in the southern Danelaw in business deals connected with Peterborough estates. The presence of a public prosecutor, or *sacrabar*, though not recorded before the Conquest seems characteristic of parts of the Danelaw, spilling over into the fringe-lands of medieval

Cheshire. The most valuable evidence comes from Ethelred's Wantage code (Ethelred III). Ethelred made reference in it to the 12 leading thegns in each wapentake in the land of the Five Boroughs who were to go from the court and to swear on relics that they would neither accuse any innocent person nor protect any guilty one. Arrangements were made for a majority decision (at least eight) in case of division of opinion among the 12. These thegns constituted a virtual jury of presentment, enjoying to all appearance an element of judgement-making greater than would be found in a normal hundred. Taken together with later urban references to lawmen or *iudices* at Cambridge, Stamford, Lincoln, York, and Chester the presence of this active jury of substantial men of a territorial neighbourhood testifies to a deep and lasting contribution on the part of the Scandinavians to the permanent legal life of England.[16]

Peculiarities in the methods of assessing fines and penalties and also in the detailed analysis of social divisions indicate some of the differences brought about by Scandinavian immigration within parts at least of the Danelaw. Antiquated units of currency (*thrymsas* in Northumbria) or Scandinavian innovations (*oras* in the territory of the Five Boroughs and the southern Danelaw generally) imply some difficulty in achieving a satisfactory basic monetary standard in the new Anglo-Scandinavian world. In Northumbria provision for a wergeld for an intermediate class of nobleman between the earls and the thegns suggest special provisions for reponsible army commanders: these men are known by the Scandinavian term 'hold'. The sustained social eminence of the free Scandinavian farmer warrior is also suggested by the simple fact that whereas in English England compensation to be paid to a lord for the death of one of his men varied in accordance with the rank of the lord, in the Danelaw the sum varied according to the dead man's status. Perhaps most important of all the technicalities is the apparent attempt to standardise fines in a way which placed a much higher premium on the king's own peace. It is always difficult to know how much weight to place on abstract legal penalties which the king would certainly have found harder to enforce in the Danelaw than in Wessex, but it does seem to be true that the king's peace (no doubt as imposed by his deputies notably in the eleventh century by the earls) was especially highly valued in the Danelaw. Efforts were also made to standardise penalties for lesser offences under the composite term *lahslit*, a penalty for the infringement of law, itself a Scandinavian word borrowed into Anglo-Saxon. Anyone who promoted an abuse, or gave a false judgement, or simply violated just law in the Danelaw was to pay *lahslit*, assessed at the high rate of ten half-marks for the king's thegn (higher in terms of silver pence than the standard English nobleman's fine of 120 shillings), six half-marks for other landowners and twelve *oras* for the freeman. Ecclesiastical offences, such as compelling a slave to work on a feast-day, refusing to pay church dues, or committing offences against a man in holy orders were also punishable by exaction of the *lahslit*. In both civil and ecclesiastical affairs the royal court was at pains to encourage rather than to suppress Danish custom. Only rarely, as when Ethelred (or more probably Archbishop Wulfstan) showed outrage at the northern custom whereby a charge of homicide brought on the day on which a victim died could not be rebutted, was any attempt made to interfere. Generally speaking Anglo-Saxon and Danish legal custom worked in reasonable harmony together.[17]

Legal innovations and modifications in methods of achieving social discipline, ecclesiastical right and a more satisfactory landlaw were perfectly acceptable in the united kingdom of Edgar and then of Cnut. A big social problem remains. Did the Danes introduce massive changes into the very social structure of England, and can the undoubted peculiarities of eastern England (when seen through western or southern eyes) be attributed directly to the Dane? There can be no doubt at all about some of the innovations. The basic field systems and methods of agriculture remained unchanged, though it is not too fanciful to suggest that some increasing efficiency, notably in the use of pasture land for sheep, may be Danish in origin. Methods of measurement of land and of assessment on the other hand were even more clearly altered. The process of change was not immediate nor was it uniform, but by the time of Domesday Book much of the Danelaw was assessed to public burdens not in terms of hides and yardlands (the customary units of English England) but in terms of carucates, or ploughlands, and of oxgangs or bovates. There may again be clues to deep social differences in these fiscal arrangements. The English divisions bore all the marks of an artificial system based ultimately on agrarian usage but weathered by long contact with government officers and landlords: a yardland was a quarter of a hide, a substantial notional stretch of territory amounting to as much as 30 acres in some parts of the country. The Danish divisions into carucates and bovates were that much nearer the soil, the ploughland representing the land that could be tilled by one plough-team in a year, the bovate or oxgang an eighth of a ploughland or the amount of land that could be apportioned to a farmer contributing one ox to the eight-ox plough-team. In at least three of the shires of the Danelaw, Nottingham, Lincolnshire and Norfolk, extending from the land of the Five Boroughs into East

Anglia, traces are to be found of a further division, Scandinavian in name and paralleled even in Normandy, possibly equivalent to the oxgang, and that is the *manslot* or portion of allotment to one free settler. Our very full records, particularly in the northern Danelaw and in parts of East Anglia, give plentiful evidence of twelfth- and thirteenth-century methods of mensuration of assessment of land that are more Scandinavian than Anglian in origin.[18]

Methods of accounting in general use in the north and east of England seem also to have been heavily affected by Scandinavian custom. A fondness for divisions into eight both in agrarian measurements and in currency was a dominant characteristic. The only current coin in the Danelaw as in English England remained the silver penny, but for accounting purposes larger amounts were assessed in terms of hundreds or 'long hundreds' of silver (equivalent in the early eleventh century to £8 in English money), marks, half-marks and *oras*. The most typical – and the most complicated – of these units was the *ora* which was generally reckoned to be worth 16 silver pennies. A mark consisted of eight *oras*, and many of the sums paid as rent for mills and fisheries in the Danelaw at the time of Domesday Book still give trace of an early and fundamental system of reckoning in these units of account of 16d. Binary reckoning came naturally to the Dane.

There remains one complicated element in the social scene that appears to offer some helpful information about the impact of the Scandinavians on English society: the nature of the peasantry in the Danelaw. Complications in interpretation occur naturally because so much of our evidence comes from Domesday Book and from later agrarian and social surveys. Throughout the Danelaw there were many marked similarities with the social structure elsewhere, with basic geographical and geological reasons determining for the most part whether or not there was a predominance of nucleated villages or hamlets or isolated farmsteads. Similar manorial arrangements were also to be found throughout England: there were lords and peasants in Dorset and in Lincolnshire. Lords, villeins, cottagers and slaves were as much a part of the social scene in Devon as in Worcester or in Yorkshire. There were, however, also some peculiarities in parts at least of the Danelaw that demand attention. English England, the south and the west, was undoubtedly more heavily manorialised than the north and the east at the time of the Norman Conquest. It was more common to find a coincidence of manor and village in English England. It was more common to find a multiplicity of manorial holdings – even up to seven or ten – in a single village in the Danelaw. In English England the manor was more firmly rooted and the lord's rights more territorialised; in the Danelaw manorial lordship and manorial rights were less onerous and more flexible. Above all there is one oddity in Domesday terminology which has occasioned much comment and discussion. The Domesday scribes used five principal terms to describe the peasantry: villeins, cottars (or bordars), slaves, freemen and sokemen. The line between freemen and sokemen is slight and hard to distinguish, connected partly with the legal obligations owed by the sokemen, partly by the legal obligations laid on the land possessed by the sokemen, and partly, one suspects, by the customs of the neighbourhood and by the scribal practice of those making the circuit returns for the Domesday Commissioners. Both groups may fairly be taken together in that they stand out against the other manorial peasantry. Freemen and sokemen had direct responsibility in matters concerning suit of court and payment of geld where the manorial peasants were fully dependent on their lords. It is the distribution of these freemen and sokemen which has prompted the deepest discussion. In substantial numbers they are to be found only north and east of Watling Street, only in other words in the Danelaw. Sokemen account for roughly half the recorded population in Lincolnshire. Freemen make up over 40 % of the recorded population in Norfolk and Suffolk. Yorkshire is a special case because of the devastation caused by William's Harrying of the North and the subsequent depreciation of peasant status, but even there firm traces remain of a greater general freedom among the peasantry. The point is firmly made by a contrast between the Domesday figures for Warwickshire and Leicestershire, counties not impossibly dissimilar in agrarian background, Warwickshire to the south and west of Watling Street in English England and its neighbour Leicestershire to the east and north in the Danelaw. Recorded populations are roughly the same, but while Leicestershire has more than a third of its population described as sokemen there are only a handful so recorded in Warwickshire. Can such a contrast be explained away as a mere difference in terminology or does it betray a social distinction of fundamental importance in the history of the English peasantry?[19]

Most historians would agree that the presence of sokemen and freemen in significant numbers does in fact betray deep differences in society, even after some discount is allowed for regional differences, such as the recording or non-recording of a free rent-paying peasantry, on the part of the Domesday scribes. Such presence points to the firmer hold of lordship on land and community in English England, and to the more intensive manorialisation of the south and west. There rests one further question vital to our present investigation, and that is quite simply how directly, if at all, is the existence of this free element in English society to be associated with the Scandinavians? Some of our finest historians have made the connection strong and direct. Sir Frank Stenton suggested that the freemen and the sokemen of the east at the time of Domesday Book were substantially the descendants of free Danish settlers, of the men of the 9th-century armies who shared out the lands of Northumbria, East Mercia and East Anglia, or of their later followers and dependants.[20] Peculiarities of land tenure, notably in East Anglia, have been associated with Scandinavian complexities where the relative freedom of a land market in newly developed territories was in conflict with Scandinavian notions of odal-right and family land. Peculiarities in definition of legal rights have been associated with the tenacity of the litigious Dane in his emphasis on the attendance of the local thing and folk-moot. Other historians have warned us instead to handle our Dane with care, to pay more attention to the question of agrarian prosperity, and to remember our ignorance of the differences in regional social structure in pre-Danish England. Some of the peculiarities of East Anglian society, for example, have been traced back to very early days and even ascribed to Frisian contacts in the days of primary Anglo-Saxon settlement. English freemen existed in significant numbers in the East Anglia of King Edmund and in the East Anglia ruled by Guthrum the converted Dane.[21] On balance it does seem desirable not to swing to an extreme nor to reject the importance of the Scandinavian element. So many fields of evidence, linguistic and social, substantiate the bare political record. It is proper however to stress that both direct and indirect effects led to the creation of the free element in the Danelaw. The direct effects are self-evident, the infusion of large numbers of Scandinavian farmer warriors with their traditions of independence, reinforced by their nature as colonists. It is doubtful, however, if these traditions would be strong enough to survive for four or five generations when subject to the political pressures and upheavals which afflicted all of Britain in the tenth and eleventh centuries. The indirect effects are a different matter. Danish conquest under Guthrum and his contemporaries brought a savage dislocation to land tenure throughout the Danelaw. Royal lands and ecclesiastical lands could not survive the onslaught. Even after the recovery and conversion in the early tenth-century royal wealth did not recover its former position and the church remained notoriously impoverished. The archbishopric of York was so poor that for two long periods it was held in plurality with the wealthy southern see of Worcester. It has long been an axiom of medieval studies that where one finds a wealthy church there also is a dependent peasantry. The dislocation caused in the Danelaw by the Danish success, no matter how swift the personal conversion, was clearly tremendous. As Christianity became again the dominant religion of the countryside so were fresh endowments made, and often – a special feature of the Danelaw – parish churches would be set up by groups of moderately prosperous freemen. By the time of the Norman Conquest the new Benedictine abbeys in the southern Danelaw and the minsters of York, Beverley, Ripon and Southwell were beginning to exhibit the features of wealthy ecclesiastical corporations. The effects of the break in continuity were nevertheless deep and enduring. At the period of growth and colonisation no well established lords, lay or ecclesiastical, were present ready and able to take the lead in new settlement and so to augment their own dominical authority. Many of the Danish army leaders, kings and jarls initially, earls and *holds* in the second phase of settlement, did extremely well out of the venture but they did not dominate the countryside as a bishop of Worcester or a great thegn or ealdorman of the south could dominate people and land. Considerable weight needs to be given to this break in the line of lordship and tenure if any full explanation of the curious social structure of the Danelaw is to be achieved.

To this point emphasis has properly been placed on Scandinavian influences on the rural society of the Danelaw. Most recent concern has centred on the problem of numbers, on the question of the density and intensity of the settlements. Were the Scandinavian elements that we can isolate so clearly in rural society the outcome of initial conquest and early heavy settlement or did they emerge as a natural product of a further period of intense colonisation in the tenth century? The balance of evidence seems at the moment to weigh in favour of the first of these two views. This is not to deny a measure, in some areas a considerable measure, of internal colonisation between 950 and 1066 A.D. by a population that can legitimately be called Anglo-Scandinavian. Monastic history as well as our more prosaic world of government activity, administration, coinage and law reminds us that the last century of Anglo-Saxon England was a time of growth and expansion internally in the economy. To go to the other extreme and to deny the presence of Scandinavian settlers in substantial numbers in the period 870–920 would seem to act against the relatively clear-cut evidence of linguistic, onomastic, institutional and indeed political history.

There remains one further important and sometimes neglected dimension to the Danish problem. Because so much of the vital evidence comes from the carefully kept records of conscientious late eleventh- and twelfth-century landlords historians have tended to concentrate on the countryside, on the Danish farmers of Yorkshire and Lincolnshire, the Grimms, Thorgeirrs, Osketills and Svartbrands of Kirkdale, Helperby, Lazenby or Conisbrough. There is therefore a danger of neglecting one of the principal contributions made by the Scandinavians, namely the stimulus given to urban development. We have from time to take talked of Danish traders, of continued contacts with the Scandinavian homeland, of continuous mobility by sea from the Northern Isles along the east coast of England to London, Kent, and round to the Isle of Wight and beyond. The tenth-century attempt to establish a kingdom with pivotal centres at Dublin and York failed: it was remarkable and significant enough that such an attempt should be made. There are consequences of all this activity which should not be ignored. Unlike the Anglo-Saxons who seemed to forget what nautical skill they ever possessed soon after landing in these islands, the Scandinavians retained their skill at sea. Their principal settlements, well fortified and under military control for at least the first generation, developed into thriving trading towns. In Northumbria York quickly grew into one of the principal urban centres of England. By the end of the Anglo-Saxon period its population approached 10,000, and indeed one contemporary source estimated the number of people in York, the 'metropolis of the Northumbrians', at an incredible (and false) figure of 30,000, not counting children and youths. The city was said to be full and wealthy beyond words with the riches of merchants who came from all sides, specially from the Danish people.[22] Lincoln also thrived mightily and under the Anglo-Scandinavian kings York and Lincoln became the administrative headquarters for the two largest shires in terms of areal extent in the whole of the English kingdom. Lincoln was one of the 'Five Boroughs', and three others, Nottingham, Derby, and Leicester also became important permanent administrative headquarters, the chief towns of their shires. The fifth of the group, Stamford, was in a special situation, something of a border borough as far as administrative arrangements were concerned, but still an important commercial centre in late Anglo-Saxon England. Further south in the Danelaw urban development was not negligible though complicated to some extent by the Benedictine revival of the late tenth century which brought ultimate importance to Peterborough, Ely, and Bury St Edmunds. Thetford, Cambridge and Norwich all show features of urban growth that owe much directly to the Scandinavian presence.

Naturally we must be careful not to attribute all urban growth to the Scandinavians. Historians are becoming increasingly aware that the second half of the tenth century and the first half of the eleventh experienced economic changes which led to the establishment of permanent town life in large tracts of the old Carolingian empire and in England. Many of the boroughs set up as defensive positions by Alfred and his son and daughter (though by no means all) also developed into English towns with permanent urban life. Fortunately we have one means of measuring the extent of Scandinavian influence on urban growth, inexact statistically but nonetheless important and significant in its way. The creation of an efficient silver coinage was one of the outstanding achievements of the late Old English monarchy. Patricularly after the reforms of Edgar the standard of the sometimes very beautiful silver pennies was systematically maintained and an elaborate administrative process established by which central royal control was imposed through issue of dies from a central die-cutting office at London, by regular changes in type of coinage, and by savage legal penalties against abuse of dies and false coining. The actual striking of coins was carried out in a multiplicity of mints (over 70 have been identified) by moneyers who were men of substance and standing, sometimes possessing their own rights of jurisdiction over dependants. These moneyers placed their own names on the reverse of the coins, together with the name of the mint. Full statistical information will be lacking until all Anglo-Saxon coins have been properly published – a massive undertaking as will be readily appreciated when it is realised that there are many thousand coins of the reign of Ethelred known from finds in the Island of Gotland alone. Statistical information, complete or incomplete, in this field has always to be handled with care: no one loses coins if he can help it and the historian can deal, unhappily, only with coins that have been lost. Even so the impressions that are already given by the samples of published coins available are so powerful that it is hard to see anything more than a spurious exactness coming from ultimate complete statistical analysis. The mints of the Danelaw contain many, often a majority, of men bearing Scandinavian names among the moneyers; in English England with few exceptions (complex London had its Scandinavian group and Chester its Irish/Norwegian elements) English names are dominant and often virtually exclusive. In sheer quantity of coins also the mints of the Danelaw contributed rather more than might be expected to the tally of surviving coins. London was undoubtedly the most prolific of the English mints and the principal trading centre. Of the next three in order of size two were Danelaw mints, York and Lincoln – and York and Lincoln contend with Winchester in the top group of mints throughout the reigns of Ethelred, Cnut and Edward the Confessor. There was also a small group of five or six prolific mints of the second order, and Stamford ranks here side by side with Chester and Bristol and Exeter and Canterbury. The evidence of the coins points unmistakeably to the importance of the Danelaw boroughs in the commercial life of England, and to the importance of a very strong Scandinavian element within the Danish boroughs.[23]

London was naturally a special case. Recent investigation, archaeological and topographical, has reinforced what the political historian has long been suggesting. The importance of London grew disproportionately to the growth of the rest of the country between say 980 and 1066. For a period of time in Alfredian England London was under Viking control and the Thames estuary continued to be an attraction for Scandinavian traders and raiders throughout the tenth century. We have seen how prominent a part London played in the Danish wars of the reign of Ethelred. Under Cnut the Scandinavians intensified their role in the trading life of the community. Viking finds, including runic inscriptions and sculpture in typical Scandinavian style, testify to their presence. The principal routine courts for handling commercial difficulties came to be known as hustings (or *hus-things*). Many early dedications to St Olaf, some of which may have been given soon after the saint's death, give positive proof of the existence of coherent groups of Scandinavians living within the city, Christian and established, yet maintaining awareness of their origins. Privileges which certainly date back to the reign of Cnut continued to be enjoyed at London by Scandinavian merchants well into the twelfth century.[24]

In conclusion it may be said that the Scandinavian impact on England resulted in a thorough enrichment of the community. Intensification of agrarian effort brought it about that by 1066 Lincolnshire, Norfolk and Suffolk ranked high among the prosperous shires of England. Scandinavian contribution to the political life of the country had been great at all levels, from the monarchy itself where Cnut ranks as one of the most successful of English rulers to the minor administrative divisions of the Danelaw and the hustings and courts of doomsmen of London, York, and Chester. The opening up of the North Sea to regular commerce proved permanent and was not disrupted by the Norman Conquest. Above all the impact of these active seafaring Northerners on the early life and stabilisation of the towns of north and eastern England was tremendous. York appears in saga stories as an impressive town where the Scandinavian language and institutions were fully familiar. The importance of the Scandinavian element in London has probably been underestimated. Regionally and generally the influx of the

Scandinavians made a vital contribution to the inner nature of the English communities of the Middle Ages.

The Celtic World

The effects of the Scandinavian invasions on the Celtic communities in Britain differed to a considerable extent from the effects on England. Accidents of geography made it more of a Norwegian venture than a Danish and there is not the same urgency for land-taking in Britain that one senses in the Danish moves. The Norwegian population was smaller and its surplus smaller still. Even so the population of Shetland alone seems to have exceeded 20,000 by the end of the Viking Age, and conservative estimates of Iceland's total population at the same period suggest a figure of over 50,000.[25] The most intense Norwegian colonising enterprises were undertaken in relation to the Northern Isles, to the Faroes, pre-eminently to Iceland and more exotically to Greenland and to Vinland on the North American coast. This sombre Northern background is forgotten at peril if one wishes to read a just evaluation of Scandinavian settlement in Celtic Britain.

The Northern Isles themselves were of course completely Scandinavianised. The language spoken in Orkney and Shetland from the end of the Viking period is generally referred to as Norn and was completely West Scandinavian, close to Norwegian. Such is the nature of island settlements that distinctions can fairly be made between the Norn of Orkney and that of Shetland, and the nature of the origin of the settlements from these distinctions. For example, while it is generally true that settlements into the northern islands came predominantly from the west and south-west coasts of Norway, Shetland Norn bears its strongest affinities with the dialects of the south-west with its focal point in the Stavanger area. Orkney Norn seems closer, though marginally only to areas a shade further east, from Stavanger to modern Kristiansand. It is a delicate point that serves to enliven the somewhat arid pages of linguistic analysis to find a conclusion that has Orkney peopled from Kristiansand and Shetland from Stavanger; and in fact language evidence, reinforced by archaeological evidence, tells us firmly that these conclusions concern only predominant groups. Norwegians from the whole littoral from Trondheim to Oslo took part in the enterprise: but the predominating element in the settlement was indeed from south-west and the west, from the Sogn and the Hardanger in particular as well as from the heartlands of Rogaland and the south.[26]

The language itself continued to dominate throughout the Middle

Ages. There was little impact from Gaelic but English (or more precisely Scottish English) began to have an influence in the later Middle Ages, probably not seriously until the fifteenth century. Political circumstances determined some change. The last of the great Norse earls was Ragnald (Rægnvold) who died in 1158, though the line lingered on until 1231. They were succeeded by Scottish earls from the mainland, of the line of Angus (1231–1321), Strathearn (1321–79) and Sinclair (from 1379). Their nominal allegiance rested with Norway, or, as it became, the joint kingdom of Norway-Denmark. We have already seen how the political links with Scandinavia were finally broken in 1468–9 when allegiance passed from Christian I of Denmark/Norway to James III of Scotland. The Sinclairs and after them the Scottish kings and earls represented a strong Scotticising agency, in the respect of language, of course, an Anglicising agent. Norn remained the common speech of Orkney throughout the sixteenth century, and the Orcadians were probably mostly bilingual throughout the seventeenth. It was not until the end of the eighteenth century that the language suffered seriously and then its disappearance was rapid. English was too strong, too useful, and too close in structure for Norn to survive into the more mobile world of the modern age. Shetland was more conservative, particularly in the remotest of the islands and as late as the 1890s Scandinavian scholars were still able to collect from living memory and use more than 10,000 words and phrases[26] of Scandinavian origin. Even more impressive is the nature of the place-name evidence. In Shetland alone the Scandinavian scholar Jakob Jakobsen, distinguished more than 50,000 names of Old Norse origin, and modern investigators put this figure as an underestimate. The overwhelming majority of historic farm-names in Orkney is of Old Norse origin, and a figure as high as 99% has been suggested and not seriously challenged. There are literally hundreds of Old Norse place-name elements to be distinguished in this mass of names. Among the most common and interesting forms, many of which are also found in mainland Britain, may be mentioned the following Old Norse elements: *bolstaðr* (farm – usually in the modern form -bister); *setr* (house or homestead); *sætr* (shieling); *staðr* (plural *staðir*: place, site, or often farm settlement, in modern place-names often reduced to -*sta* or -*ster* or in Orkney modified to -*ston*); *borg* (a fortification); *by(r)* (in the Northern Isles 'farm' not as in the Danelaw from Danish -*by* meaning 'village'); *skali* (hut or shed, but often in Orkney 'hall'); *kvi* (enclosure for cattle – in modern form – quoy); *garðr* (enclosure). Natural features and especially words connected with the sea and the coast are of almost exclusively Old

Norse origin (for example the familiar *ey* (island), *nes* (promontory), and *vik* (bay or inlet), and the not quite so familiar *hamarr* (rock, wall of rock), *mynni* (mouth of river), and *vagr* (creek or bay as in modern Kirkwall or Osmundwall or Snarravoe).[27]

Institutional evidence confirms, if confirmation is needed, the story told by the structure of the language and the place-names. Methods of settling local disputes, the solemn rules of the assemblies or 'things', the system of taxation based closely on Norwegian practice, the units of taxation and the terminology, the equation of the proceeds of taxation with provision of ships for defence are only a few among the many institutional features of the Northern Isles that tell of Scandinavian customs and Scandinavian inhabitants. Strong though it is the institutional evidence needs to be handled with care. Our knowledge of it comes from later sources and there is a sense in which it is particularly naïve to express surprise that communities that bore allegiance to Scandinavian kings and princes for over half a millennium should enjoy a Scandinavian type of institutional life. The economy was similar, the social life based on the sea and the sheep-farm almost identical. Special characteristics, such as the nature of the water-mills tell also of a Norwegian affinity. Taken together with the language and the place-names the institutions of Orkney and Shetland point to one inescapable conclusion. The Northern Isles represent in their medieval being a firm testimony to the success of a colonising venture undertaken by Norwegians in the Viking Age, on a par with the settlement of the Faroes and of Iceland, a touchstone and a contrast to the rest of Britain.

For when we turn to the rest of the Celtic World, the mainland of much of the Highlands of Scotland, the Hebrides, the southern Scottish islands, part of the mainland of south-west Scotland, the Isle of Man, Ireland and Wales, we find plentiful evidence of Scandinavian presence but nothing resembling the complete Scandinavianisation so characteristic of Orkney and Shetland. We miss the clearcut language evidence of Norn and face difficulties different in kind but as great in their way as those that faced us in consideration of the impact of Scandinavian language elements on English. Again, however, language and place-names offer the first field for examination, and it is already true to say that the efforts of three or four generations of devoted students of the Celtic languages are beginning to make the long-lasting effects of Viking adventure and Scandinavian settlement more intelligible. The Celtic languages are very different in structure, vocabulary and stress from the Germanic. Wherever a sizeable population survived (in other words virtually everywhere in the Celtic West) the native language tended to survive side by side with Scandinavian in clear duality rather than in symbiosis. Even so the effects of the presence of Scandinavian speakers had varying impact on the Celtic-speaking communities, and the many variations themselves tell us much of the degree of Scandinavian influence.

It is now generally agreed that Scottish Gaelic is directly descended from the language spoken by immigrants into Argyll from north-east Ireland (Dalriada) towards the end of the 5th century A.D. There was no serious divergence from the language of the Irish homeland until at least the tenth century, and most would say that even as late as the thirteenth century they were still essentially one language, common Gaelic as it is sometimes called. This is not to say that there was not intense local divergence in speech from part to part of the Gaelic-speaking world, but essentially there was only one language in that world throughout the Middle Ages. As Professor Jackson has shown us in a famous and fundamental lecture, 'until at least the end of the sixteenth century Ireland and the Highlands formed a single culture-province'.[28] Their unity was demonstrated and to some extent preserved by the attachment of the learned literate classes to the common Gaelic tongue, admittedly as the early modern period progressed more and more a literary language increasingly antiquated and divorced from the living, diverging, spoken Gaelic tongues of Ireland and Scotland. The Gaelic tongue of Man was part of the unified group and its spoken version continued to be close to Scottish Gaelic certainly until the end of the Middle Ages. Dramatic sound changes in the 5th and 6th centuries and less spectacular modifications up to at least 1000 A.D. were shared in common by the whole group. Differentiations, mostly in the degree to which changes were accepted, begin to occur between the tenth and the thirteenth centuries and slowly a spoken Eastern Gaelic (Scottish and Manx) comes to be distinguished from Western Gaelic or Irish. After the thirteenth century the two groups cease to share innovation in common except for rare coincidence and after the fifteenth century Eastern Gaelic sees further decisive differentiation within itself between Scottish Gaelic and Manx.[29]

We now have to face directly the very complicated question of Norse influence on Gaelic. Language in this respect mirrors faithfully political developments. The Norwegian king, Magnus Barefoot, had asserted his lordship over Shetland, Orkney, the Hebrides, Anglesey and Man in the course of his dramatic and full-scale expedition of 1098 to which we have previously made reference. Not all his gains were permanent, but he made a treaty with Edgar, king of the Scots (1097–1107) which provided the formal basis for the constitutional situation in the islands for much of the Middle Ages. Magnus was recognised as lord of the isles with the right to the allegiance of the local rulers. He made no claim to the mainland (apart from Kintyre), although there were Norse rulers in much of the North, in Caithness, Ross, and Sutherland. It is not too much to say that the main lines of political development in the succeeding century and a half consisted of Scottish attempts with reasonable success to make a reality of their lordship of the North and Norwegian failure to make a reality of their lordship of the West. The independence of the 'kings' of the islands became legendary, though from time to time the lordship of Norway in civil matters concerning tribute and in ecclesiastical matters (particularly after the setting up of the archbishopric at Nidaros in the early 1150s) was fully recognised. Haakon IV in 1266 made one final effort to impose strong Norwegian control, was defeated by the Scottish king (and the weather) at the battle of Largs in the October and died in Orkney on his way home. The resulting Treaty of Perth set the seal on island constitutional history for the succeeding two centuries. The Hebrides and the Isle of Man passed into Scottish hands in return for a payment of 4,000 marks and an annual render of 100 marks. Scottish lordship did not in point of fact prove much more effective than Norwegian. The Isle of Man passed into English control in the fourteenth century. In the Islands themselves authority rested with the lords of the isles, chieftains (MacDougalls and later MacDonalds) in direct descent from the twelfth-century Scandinavian adventurer and jarl Somerled. Effective Scottish control had to wait in large measure until the sophisticated days of James VI (James I of England) in the early seventeenth century. [30]

During all these centuries of turmoil there was constant contact between Gaelic and Scandinavian speakers. There was a long bilingual period which lasted certainly to the thirteenth century and probably longer. In the event the Norsemen became Gaelic-speakers in the Hebrides and also where they settled in the Highlands. It seems likely (and this again makes sound political sense) that the thirteenth century was the decisive point in which Eastern Gaelic separated off from Western. And the Norse influence, especially in place-names and in general vocabulary, is one of the distinguishing marks between Eastern and Western Gaelic, between Scottish and Irish. The vast majority of the present Gaelic place-names in the Outer Hebrides, especially Lewis, are of ultimate Norse origin. In the Inner Hebrides the proportion is still high and has been estimated at 60% in Skye and about a third in Islay. The contrast with Ireland in this respect is startling, for hardly any Norse names of Irish places have been taken over into Irish. On the mainland of Scotland they have left evidence of their presence both in pure Norse forms and in forms that have been taken over into Gaelic: *ob* (bay), *vidh* (a ford), *dail* (field), *sgol* (rinse or wash), *strome* (a current or stream), are among the most obvious of the place-name elements. Borrowings into vocabulary include common words such as *lagh* (law), *nabaidh* (neighbour), *stailinn* (steel), *biota* (a churn), and *geodha* (a creek): these are common to Manx as well as to Scottish but do not appear in Irish. Some of the most intimate and intricate sound changes, common to Scottish Gaelic and Manx, seem also attributable to Old Norse influence, including vowel-shortening which brought the stress-system of Scottish Gaelic 'into still closer conformity with that of Old Norse'.[31] The Isle of Man was a special case, and Manx Gaelic suffered severely from heavy Anglo-Norman pressure throughout the critical twelfth and thirteenth centuries; even so a sizeable minority of Manx place-names (probably about one in six) are wholly or partly of ultimate Scandinavian origin, and the vocabulary of Manx Gaelic has preserved a few Scandinavian borrowings (*spret* (start), *grinney* (a gate), and *oalsun* (a rope from head to foreleg of a cow)) not to be found in its Scottish sister language. Brilliant archaeological work in Man which has made us familiar with Viking boat-shaped long-houses, with Viking graves (including the important boat burial at Balladoole), and Viking ornamentation in the full Ringerike and Urnes styles, has made the Scandinavian presence tangible and intelligible as in few parts of the British Isles. The practice of boat burial, not commonly recorded in the British Isles, and even a possible example of suttee remind us of the intensity of the social impact from an early stage. On the whole the evidence is consistent for Man as for the Hebrides and the Highlands. Gaelic and Scandinavian languages were spoken in close conjunction for at least four centuries and had important structural influences the one on the other.[32]

Institutional evidence for the impact of Scandinavian settlement is also plentiful along the Celtic West. Again the Northern Isles are in a category of their own, their institutional life thoroughly Scandinavian in all respects. They provide the centre and focal point for all moves to a more thorough political and social Scandinavianisation of the western seaboard of Britain. On the mainland of Scotland effects were more spasmodic and less long-lasting. The name Dingwall (*Thing-vollr*, place of assembly and presumably administrative headquarters) serves to remind us that at its height Scandi-

navian political influence was paramount throughout much of Scotland to the north of the Great Glen. Dingwall is no more than a dozen miles from modern Inverness. The north-east Scottish coast was surely the preserve of Scandinavian fleets ranging from the Northern Isles base, and for a long period a Scandinavian jarl exercised authority in Caithness, at times subservient to the earls of the isles, at times virtually independent, and at other times again subordinate if not subservient to the Scottish kings. The mainland, however, came fully under Scottish control before the end of the Middle Ages with the result that fewer signs are to be found there than in the isles of Scandinavian institutional influence. Elsewhere it is a different matter. The taxation system and accompanying administrative divisions established in the Viking Age and confirmed and reinforced by Norwegian kings and earls in the twelfth and thirteenth century have left a permanent mark on the Northern and Western Isles and Man. In constitutional theory they were administered by the earl of Orkney who exacted tribute, two-thirds of which was to go to the king while he (or men acting for him) was to take the other third. This overall scheme was common to the Scandinavian world, and analogies have been found with the Baltic earldoms, especially on the Isle of Gotland, that were subordinate to the Swedish crown.[33] Even more striking analogies have been found with the administrative systems erected to make the tribute-taking possible. They are clearly related to the familiar Norwegian institution of *leidung*, that is to say a taxation system arranged so as to provide the lord and ruler with a suitable well-manned, and well-equipped fleet. Orkney for example was divided into six districts called *husaby* districts, with a *husaby* estate in each, that is to say a farm to which tribute would be brought in proper season. The *husaby* districts were further divided into thirty-six units called *urisland*, and they in turn were subdivided into quarters known as *skattlands*. The system seems complicated but may in fact have been simple and effective. The name *skattland* (scot-paying land) is in itself revealing and represents the basic family farm set up when free settlers took land. Each *husaby* district in Orkney contained 144 *skattlands* which may well have been referred to as a 'long hundred' (a duodecimal 'hundred' of 12 × 12).[34] It is further possible that the 144 tax-paying units went to further the construction and maintenance of four ships (with 36 oars apiece): in origin at least levy service would be expected from each of these basic units. If we turn to the bigger unit, the *urisland*, again the term itself is informative. It means literally an 'ounce' land, that is to say territory contributing a standard ounce of silver at the time of the annual levying of tax or tribute. From the central earldom of Orkney this would amount to 144 ounces of silver to the Norwegian king a year and 72 ounces to the earl. Relationship with the systems in force in the Scandinavian homeland is direct and immediate, but recent investigation has enabled us to take the story further. In spite of differences in terminology the taxation and administrative systems in force in the Hebrides and in the Isle of Man appear to have been identical. In the Hebrides divisions known as *tirungs* corresponded to the *urislands* and they again were divided into quarters. In the Isle of Man the analogy is even more exact. The island was divided into six sheadings (an Old West Scandinavian word *settungr*, a sixth). Each sheading was divided into 36 *treens* and these again were split up into four *quarterlands*. The *quarterland* (like the *skattland*) constituted the basic unit of levy. It may well be also, an analogy with Scandinavian custom, that the *treens* (or *urislands* or *tirungs*) had the basic responsibility in the early days of the conversion for the provision of a small chapel (or *Keill*) and that this responsibility later developed into the duty of looking after parts of the bigger churches which in time replaced the early chapels. Some of these administrative arrangements may be traced back to pre-Viking days and indeed be fundamental to the first ordering of territorial government in the Scottish kingdom of the 9th century. But it would seem rash to deny the Norseman a major part in the final shaping of the government system of administration and taxation in the lands which lay completely under their nominal control until at least 1266.

Ireland

The Irish situation is different in nature and in degree from the Scottish and the Manx. The defeat at Clontarf in 1014 did not lead to the expulsion of the Scandinavians. They continued to live and trade and fight and even to recruit from Scandinavia proper and from the Islands. Clontarf nevertheless had a direct effect on their development. The defeat marks an end of any Scandinavian hopes (no matter how fleeting and illusory) of forming a coherent territorial kingdom or earldom that would incorporate large tracts of countryside. It marks a decisive stage in the localisation of Scandinavian settlement in Ireland.

There were, of course, indications even before Clontarf that this was a strong element in Irish/Scandinavian history. Expansionist schemes in the tenth century had been directed strongly eastwards across the Irish Sea into north-west England and over the Pennines to York. In no part of Europe – though there are possible analogies

along the Waterways of Russia – did the Vikings concentrate so clearly on their fortified settlements and quaysides along the coast. Dublin, Waterford, Wexford, Cork and Limerick remained their headquarters, sometimes under Scandinavian dynasties, sometimes subject directly to native Irish rulers. After the Anglo-Norman Conquest in the early 1170s these settlements were subsumed in the greater Angevin empire. The Ostmen (men from the east) enjoyed a precarious independence in social matters for another century or so but were of no further consequence in the political history of Ireland.

The direct effects of the Vikings on Irish society are therefore not as great as one might expect. They have left a scatter of vocabulary, notably in matters concerning the sea and ships and commerce, but not nearly as much as in Scottish Gaelic. Indeed some of the Norse influence on Irish Gaelic has been explained by immigration from the Islands and the Highlands across the North Channel into Ulster and the north-east as far south as Louth and North Meath. Language authorities date these modifications primarily to the period between the fourteenth and the end of the sixteenth century. Norse influence on place-names is also relatively localised, again much less widespread and deep than in the Scottish Gaelic areas.[35]

We must not nevertheless attempt to underwrite and to minimise the indirect effects of the Vikings. We have seen already how politically they helped to accelerate a natural movement in balance from the centre towards the east. Throughout the century and a half that separated Clontarf from the Anglo-Norman invasion they remained a dominant power on the Irish Sea. They were the great traders of the western seaboard during this age. Their coinage, modelled on English example in the last decade of the tenth century, helped to formalise and ease trading ventures from Ireland into England, particularly along their two well-beaten routes that led to Chester and to Bristol. Dublin, Wexford and Waterford provided important staging points that linked the mobile men of the North with settled England. Above all there should be no denigration of the part they played in increasing the wealth of Ireland and in establishing firmly the beginnings of urban institutional life. As specialist boat-builders, sailors and traders they seem to have been somewhat encapsulated as far as ordinary Irish society was concerned. Excavation by archaeologists, notably in High Street and Winetavern Street, Dublin, has helped to give a realistic picture of the state of urban material development, enough to indicate that a high degree of material comfort had been achieved.[36]

The ecclesiastical life of Ireland was radically altered in the course of the late eleventh and early twelfth centuries; and the coastal settlements played a vital part in events that led to a measure of reform and a complete overhaul of the diocesan system. English influences came in heavily through the Scandinavian towns, especially through Dublin. Lanfranc, archbishop of Canterbury (1070–89) took it as a vital part of his duty to extend as far as it was possible the hold of his metropolitan church over the Irish Christians, and it was the see of Dublin that saw the strongest of his ventures. Bishop Patrick (d. 1084) was consecrated by Lanfranc and so was his successor Donatus (d. 1095). Archbishop Anselm had the same basic aspirations and consecrated Bishop Samuel (d. 1121). Oaths of obedience were exacted from these men in conformity to the custom of Canterbury. Anselm further consecrated Malchus as the first bishop of Waterford in 1096. All these men were Irishmen trained in England, and at a great reforming Synod held in 1111 it is notable that Dublin was not included among the Irish sees because its bishops were subject to Canterbury. Ecclesiastical practice in this respect surely reflected social reality. The world of the Hiberno-Norse townsmen and traders was more akin to England than to Gaelic Ireland. Reform came to the Irish church partly through the Hiberno-Norse bishops but partly also through sheer pressure of Hildebrandine ideas largely disseminated through the English church. Both Lanfranc and Anselm were concerned, as their voluminous correspondence shows, with the state of the Irish church. Charges of laxness in the imposition of marriage laws, of the uses in procedures for episcopal consecration and of church ceremony were freely made. By the early twelfth century the Papacy itself was represented by its own legate, possibly first by Ua-Dunain, the bishop of the Meath, and thereafter certainly by Gilbert, bishop of Limerick who resigned his charge to St Malachy in 1140. At the Synod of Kells in 1152, Dublin itself was brought fully into the Irish fold and recognised as an archbishopric under the primacy of Armagh. Cardinal John Paparo brought *pallia* for the former archbishops, Armagh, Cashel, Dublin, and Tram, with express recognition of the primacy of Armagh. Canterbury had indeed failed to secure permanent control, but its influence, particularly through the Hiberno-Norse bishoprics, was considerable.[37]

In spite of the obvious importance of the Hiberno-Norse element in commercial and religious life it remains true to say that the ultimate impact of the Vikings on the political moulding of Ireland remained less formidable than on Man, the Islands and the Highlands. The reason for this is partly to be found in the later chequered history of Ireland. The Anglo-Norman conquest of more than half

the island brought about changes, in language, social structure and religious organisations that in one respect consummated the possible patterns hinted at in Hiberno-Norse developments and completely overshadowed it. Most of all however the reason is to be found in the nature of the settlements themselves. During these centuries permanence went with the land. The traders and sailors of Dublin and Waterford did not bring the permanent marks of the settler and coloniser into Irish society.

Wales

The effects of the Viking invasions on Wales present a different picture again from that which we have seen elsewhere in the Celtic world. There are resemblances to the situation in Ireland but there is one big contrast. There is no certain evidence that a substantial Viking fortified centre on the scale of Dublin or Waterford was established in Wales. It is possible, indeed probable, that for substantial periods of time Norse-speaking men built up settlements that were meant to be permanent in Pembrokeshire and in several favoured seaports along the South Welsh coast; but these were small-scale, purposeful, almost one might say vocational. They were connected with Hiberno-Norse control of sea-routes and trading ventures into England by means of the Bristol Channel. Even more so than in Ireland the seamen lacked a territorial base. There was no mastery of the hinterland and without that permanent impress was impossible in the Viking centuries.

The reasons for this state of affairs are relatively simple to analyse and we have already in an earlier chapter discussed the political situation which led to successful Welsh resistance at critical moments when serious colonising settlement might have been attempted. Indeed if the full perspective of Scandinavian settlement is taken into account it will readily be seen that the colonising thrust necessarily grows weaker the further south the longships have to travel. There was only a limited supply of manpower. Along the south-western route the Norwegians settled lustily in the Northern Isles, the Hebrides, and Man. Ireland attracted but in the end at Clontarf repelled; and the Welsh situation was even more unfavourable without adequate human resources to sustain it. From time to time and most notably at the very end of the Viking Age proper attempts were made to bring at least Anglesey fully into the Hiberno-Norse world. Long tradition, association with Man (the Menevian islands of antiquity), accessibility from Dublin, and normal mastery of northern waters prompted Magnus Barefoot of Norway to make his last great demonstration in 1098. Demonstration is the right word; there was no colonising stuffing to give it permanent strength.

The results are calculable. There is virtually no significant Scandinavian element in the Welsh language. A few common words which may easily have infiltrated through English – such as *iarll*, the Welsh equivalent of 'earl' – are all that one can point to with certainty. Attempts to suggest that some dialectical changes in the Welsh of the north-west or of the south-west may be due to Scandinavian influence have not been successful. Neither is there any substantial evidence in favour of institutional change that can properly be attributed to Scandinavian influence, apart perhaps from a certain legal flexibility and willingness to borrow from Anglo-Saxon legal sources prompted in the tenth century by the sheer menace of heathen attack. Very close and careful work on the agrarian structure of medieval Pembrokeshire has failed utterly to disclose anything in the social patterns that can be squared sensibly with the institutions of the Danelaw or the Danicised segments of Normandy. In the last resort the case for Scandinavian settlement in Wales rests on interpretation given to difficult narrative sources and to place-names, supplemented to some extent even by some rather unusual blood-group characteristics discovered by investigations in parts of Pembrokeshire.[38]

Most of the narrative sources, the Lives of the Saints, the Annals and the Anglo-Norman historiography concentrate on dramatic incidents, raids on churches, pillage and rapine, usually by Scandinavians operating well within the Hiberno-Norse circuit. By the end of the eleventh century and the beginning of the twelfth Dublin naval power is an important factor in the general political life of Wales. There is however no explicit reference to Viking settlements in Wales. The most interesting accounts came from later Scandinavian tradition, above all from the *Jomsvikingasaga* which has a series of references to a presumably Danish colony set up in *Bretland* into which the founder of Jomsborg, Palnatoki, is said to have married. The stories are circumstantial, tell of the establishment of Norsemen in significant numbers even before Palnatoki's first visit (*c.* 930–5), and of the continued existence of the colony throughout the tenth century. We have learned to handle the Jomsvikings with care, and Palnatoki with the utmost scepticism, but there is still interest in the fact that the good twelfth-century storyteller considered that it would not strain the credulity of his readers too far to hear of a Scandinavian kingdom in Wales (always assuming they identified *Bretland* as Wales).[39] Evidence from place-names and from genealogies is too intangible and has to be forced too hard to make a strong case for associating any specific Viking leader or group with any specific area of Wales. If they did indeed found a more or less permanent settlement in Wales it is likely that it was in the south-west around Milford Haven; but beyond that it would be rash to go. Vikings as we know in the Alfredian period moved easily from the South Welsh coast into Devon and Somerset. A permanent base in the south-west would have been convenient; but tenth-century equivalents of Waterford or Wexford in Pembrokeshire are no more than hypotheses based on no hard evidence.

The clearest signs of Scandinavian presence in Wales come from place-names, mostly recorded naturally enough in the early stages in English or Latin forms, underlining the complicating factor in all place-name studies that we have so often to take into account the date and language of their first record, both of which can be very different from the date and language of first naming.[40] Things are especially complicated in the Bristol Channel area where the place of first record must often have been the ports, especially Bristol and Dublin rather than the hinterland of the Carmarthenshire or Glamorganshire or Monmouthshire countryside. The vast majority of Scandinavian place-names consist of navigation points and of the names of small islands which themselves could have been previously navigation points. In the north Bardsey (known consistently and unwaveringly in Welsh as Ynys Enlli), Piscar, Holyhead, the Skerries, Priestholm, and Orme's Head fall into this category. Anglesey (consistently Mon in Welsh), meaning Ongull's island, is more difficult to understand. If, as seems certain, it bears the Scandinavian personal name Ongull there follows a natural assumption that a settlement was made at least on part of the island, presumably at Holyhead, and was in the possession of a Scandinavian community long enough for the name to become current in Chester and Dublin. The name 'Anglesey' is first recorded by the Anglo-Saxon Chronicle in 1098 in connection with Magnus Barefoot's expedition, and twelfth-century belief that both the main Menevian islands, Man and Anglesey, were then known as the islands 'of the English' (*insulae Anglorum*) seems to have been ill-founded. The name 'Anglesey' certainly presents problems, and may suggest at least a temporary establishment of a Scandinavian fortified post in the island. It is unthinkable however that a substantial and enduring colonisation took place in this most Welsh of all Welsh communities, *Môn Mam Cymru, Mona*, the mother of Wales.

In the south there is a similar preponderance of navigation point and small island names, again with one or two crucial puzzles. Ramsey, Emsgar, Skomer, Skokholm, Grassholm, Gateholm,

Midland (Middelholm) Island, the Tusker Rocks, Stack Rocks, Caldy, Goskar, Burry Holm, Sker, Rothers Sker, and the two holms at the narrow neck of the Channel between East Glamorgan and Somerset, Flat Holm and Steep Holm, fit easily into this category. There are also clusters of names (unfortunately difficult to date precisely) which suggest something more than a sailor's record. In Pembrokeshire Milford Haven (recorded in the late twelfth and early thirteenth centuries as *Milver* and *Mellferth*) is derived from the Scandinavian *fjorðr*, fjord, a good topographical description. Fishguard (*fiskrgarðr* 'fishyard'), Amroth, Colby, Freystrop, Gelliswick, Goultrop, Hasguard, Lydstep, Musselwick and Steynton, all contain probable Scandinavian elements, and some of these places lie inland of the haven. The situation is obscured (as in Ireland) by the Anglo-Norman settlement of Pembroke and the importation of Flemish settlers but there still remains a reasonable case for the physical presence of Scandinavians, colonising tracts of country behind their main base and navigation centre, the great fjord of Milford. Most but not all (Fishguard itself is a notable exception) apparent Scandinavian settlements lie to the south of the Anglo-Welsh linguistic division which, following the line of early Norman castles from west to east of the shire, is known to this day as the land-share or land-boundary.

Further east than Pembrokeshire there is also some evidence of Scandinavian influence away from the waters of the Channel. There are Scandinavian names in the princely genealogies of Ystradtawe. Some of the great stone crosses on the Pembrokeshire/Carmarthen border – Nevern and Penally – have marked Scandinavian features. In Glamorgan and especially around Cardiff there are some inland Scandinavian settlement names (Womanby Street in Cardiff (Hundmanby), and Lamby and Homri). But these could be a product of the Anglo-Scandinavian world rather than the Hiberno-Norse: *Hundmanby* is a known form in Yorkshire and the evidence from artistic features would well point to the Danelaw rather than to Ireland. The name Swansea (Sweynesse – probably Sweyn's island) is unquestionably Scandinavian. Worm's Head, on the other hand, is an English form (dragon's head) in contrast to the Norse dragon's head of the north at Orme's Head.

The most that one can do is to try to give a possible interpretation of this difficult evidence in full realisation that some of the material may indeed be too ambiguous to bear a heavy weight of synthesis. We have no coins to help us since the littoral distribution of coin hoards in Wales is absolute. It is however certain that Scandinavian sailors were active at an early stage in the Bristol Channel and it is quite possible that in the tenth century they set up trading posts in Pembrokeshire and perhaps further east. Indeed one can go further and suggest that they were responsible for the first effective and permanent opening-up of the trading routes from Ireland to Bristol and from Ireland to Chester. They named the navigation points and staging posts in their Scandinavian tongue, and repeated them in that form to the Anglo-Saxon world and to the Anglo-Norman world of 1066–1154. By that time they had probably had an active part to play in the establishment of Bristol and the growth of Chester. There is little evidence of permanent agrarian settlement except, as we have seen, in south Pembrokeshire and possibly in and behind Cardiff and Swansea. The great task of the Scandinavians was the concentration on continuous navigation in both principal routes to England from the Irish coast, that is to say the route to Bristol and the route to Chester; and it is quite possible that they set up their fortified harbours and quays in Milford, in Cardiff and in Swansea as a means of ensuring permanent life to those routes. The most likely period for the realisation of permanent settlement of this type could well be the period of relative lull in pirate activity, in the middle years of the tenth century. Progress and development coincided with the rise of Bristol, 990–1040. Agrarian hinterland was of secondary importance even in Pembrokeshire and certainly in Anglesey. Continuous navigation was the aim and the achievement. Such a picture is conjectural but it makes sense. The native Welsh community was relatively untouched except for the disasters to ecclesiastical life that came from occasional raiding. In the north apart from some spill-over into the north-east of Wales from the Wirral and Anglo-Scandinavian Cheshire there was no significant agrarian settlement. The Scandinavians were bent on stabilising routes not on setting up colonies. It is as part of the evolution of the Hiberno-Norse merchant endeavour that Scandinavian impact on Wales must be read.

References

Chapter 1

1. H. R. LOYN and J. PERCIVAL, *The Reign of Charlemagne*, London, 1975, pp. 3–5.

1. R. I. PAGE, *An Introduction to English Runes*, London, 1973, provides a reliable and readable guide to the study of runes and runic alphabets.

3. E. V. GORDON, *An Introduction to Old Norse*, Oxford, 1927 (2nd rev. ed. by A. R. Taylor, 1957), provides a reliable guide to the language for English-speaking readers.

4. GWYN JONES, *A History of the Vikings*, Oxford, 1968, p. 110.

5. H. H. LAMB, *Climate Present, Past, and Future*, vol. i (Fundamentals and Climate Now), London, 1972, and also ch. 5 (Climatic Fluctuations) in *General Climatology*, vol. ii, ed. H. Flohn, Amsterdam, 1969, p. 182.

6. A good discussion of the Greenland settlement is given by Gwyn Jones, *op. cit.*, pp. 306–11 and *The Norse Atlantic Saga*, Oxford, 1964.

7. The seminal article of Gustaf Utterström, 'Climatic Fluctuations and Population Problems in Early Modern History', *Scandinavian Econ. H.R.*, iii, 1955, retains its importance for the Viking period. S. Bolin, 'Mohammed, Charlemagne, and Ruric', *ibid.*, i, 1953, is also relevant and important.

8. PETER SAWYER, *The Age of the Vikings* (2nd ed.), London, 1971, pp. 68–76: ch. 4 'The Ships' (pp. 66–85) with critical and up-to-date notes (to 1971) remains the best short introduction in English to Viking ships.

9. GWYN JONES, *A History of the Vikings*, pp. 190–4, and Jacqueline Simpson, *Everyday Life in the Viking Age*, London, 1967, pp. 94–5. A curious reference to navigation instruments, destruction of which led to the foundering of a Viking fleet in the Bristol Channel, occurs in the late-eleventh century Life of St Gwynllyw, *Lives of Cambro-British Saints*, ed. W. J. Rees, Llandovery, 1853, pp. 151–3.

Chapter 2

1. L. MUSSET, *Les Invasions: le Second Assaut contre l'Europe Chrétienne* (*VIIIᵉ–XIᵉ siècles*), Paris, 1965.

2. R. H. M. DOLLEY, *Anglo-Saxon Pennies*, London, 1964, gives the best short introduction to the staple coinage of the period. C. H. V. Sutherland, *English Coinage*, London, 1973, with selective bibliography, provides a general account. For Offa's coinage, C. E. Blunt's essay 'The coinage of Offa' is indispensable; it appears in the important volume of essays written in tribute to Sir Frank Stenton: *Anglo-Saxon Coins*, ed. R. H. M. Dolley, London, 1961.

3. SIR FRANK STENTON gives the best appraisal of Offa's achievements, *Anglo-Saxon England*, Oxford, 1943 (3rd ed. 1971), ch. VII 'The Ascendancy of the Mercian Kings'.

4. A. A. M. DUNCAN, *Scotland, the Making of the Kingdom*, Edinburgh, 1975, pp. 94–8, gives a reasoned and convincing analysis of the tangle of events in the tenth and early eleventh centuries.

5. KATHLEEN HUGHES, *The Church in Early Irish Society*, London, 1966, especially pp. 197–202.

Chapter 3

1. G. STORM (ed.), *Historia Norvegiae*, Oslo, 1880, pp. 88–90, quoted and paraphrased by Wainwright in F. T. Wainwright (ed.) *The Northern Isles*, London, 1962, p. 99.

2. A. W. BRÖGGER, *Ancient Emigrants*, Oxford, 1929, pp. 56–67): Wainwright, *op. cit.*, p. 101.

3. A. A. M. DUNCAN, *Scotland, the Making of the Kingdom*, Edinburgh, 1975, ch. iv 'Lochlannaich, Cuimrich, Sassunaich'. Reference to Dr Ritchie's work at Buckquoy is given on p. 82.

4. J. R. C. HAMILTON, *Excavations at Jarlshof*, Edinburgh, 1956, and 'Jarlshof, A Prehistoric and Viking Settlement in Shetland', *Recent Archaeological Excavations in Britain*, ed. R. L. S. Bruce-Mitford, London, 1956, provides the essential analysis of this important site.

5. A. P. SMYTH, *Scandinavian York and Dublin*, Dublin, 1975, brings evidence to suggest that the 'grandsons of Ivar, including Ragnall (d. 920), Sihtric (d. 927) and Olaf's father, Guthfrith (d. 934) were indeed grandsons of Ivar the Boneless (d. 873).

6. *English Historical Documents*, vol. i, ed. D. Whitelock, London, 1953 (E.H.D. i), pp. 775–7. Letter to Ethelred, king of Northumbria.

7. ed. D. WHITELOCK, *The Anglo-Saxon Chronicle*, London, 1961. The main structure of the narrative account of Alfred's reign depends heavily on the Chronicle account together with material from Asser – much of which is brought to attention by Professor Whitelock's footnotes.

8. R. H. M. DOLLEY, *Anglo-Saxon Pennies*, London, 1964, p. 20.

9. DAVID WILSON, 'The Vikings' Relationship with Christianity in Northern England' *Journal of the British Archaeological Association*, 1967, and 'Archaeological Evidence for the Viking Settlements and Raids in England', *Frühmittelalterliche Studien* 2, 1968, are both important.

10. DOROTHY WHITELOCK, 'The conversion of the Eastern Danelaw', *Saga-Book of the Viking Society*, 1941.

11. 'The Danes in England', *Proceedings of the British Academy*, 1928, p. 204–5.

12. SIR FRANK STENTON, *Anglo-Saxon England*, Oxford, 3rd ed., 1971, p. 349: William of Malmesbury, *Gesta Regum*, vol. i Rolls Series, London, 1887, p. 149.

13. A. CAMPBELL (ed.), *The Battle of Brunanburh*, London, 1938.

Chapter 4

1. D. M. WILSON and OLE KLINDT-JENSEN, *Viking Art*, London, 1966, plates XLVIII and XLIX, and pp. 119–22.

2. GWYN JONES, *A History of the Vikings*, pp. 360–4 provides an attractive and clear description of Trelleborg together with a plan (p. 361) of the camp. Olaf Olsen 'The Geometrical Viking Fortresses', *Château Gaillard* IV, ed. A. L. J. van de Walle, Ghent, 1968, pp. 185–90, comments on the geometrical precision of the sites, rampart, ditch, and lay-out within the rampart. Else Roesdahl 'The Viking Fortress of Fyrkat in the light of the objects found', *Château Gaillard* VI, ed. M. de Bouard, Caen, 1973, pp. 196–202, favours a function more complicated than that of mere barracks for the fortresses. There is an important article on 'The Trelleborg House Reconsidered' by Holger Schmidt, *Medieval Archaeology* 17 (1973), pp. 52–77.

3. DAG STRÖMBÄCH, *The Conversion of Iceland*, London, 1975, gives the best critical account of the sources for the conversion, pp. 13–26. J. Brøndsted, *The Vikings*, Penguin Books, London, 1960, 2nd ed. 1965, p. 85.

4. PETER SAWYER, *The Age of the Vikings*, ch. 5 'Treasure', especially pp. 117–18. R. H. M. Dolley, 'Some Reflections on Hildebrand Type A of Ethelred II', *Antikvariskt Arkiv* 9, Stockholm, 1958, and *The Hiberno-Norse Coins in the British Museum*, London, 1966, makes valuable contribution to knowledge and understanding of the situation. See also Sawyer's references to the work of Sture Bolin and Nils Rasmusson among others.

5. SVEN JANSSON, *Swedish Vikings in England: the Evidence of the Rune Stones*, (Dorothea Coke Memorial Lecture, University College, London), 1966.

Chapter 5

1. *Sweet's Anglo-Saxon Reader* rev. ed. by D. Whitelock, Oxford, 1967, p. 126, gives a reliable text: a good translation appears in E.H.D. i, pp. 293–7.

2. F. LIEBERMANN, *Die Gesetze der Angelsachsen*, i, Hallé, 1903, new impression Tübingen, 1960, pp. 220–7; E.H.D. i, pp. 401–02.

3. FLORENCE OF WORCESTER, *Chronicon ex Chronicis*, ed. B. Thorpe, London, vol. i, 1848.

4. *The Anglo-Saxon Chronicle*, ed. D. Whitelock, (with David Douglas and Susie Tucker), London, 1961 (a revised version of the translation contained in the first two volumes of E.H.D.), s.a. 994.

5. *ibid.*, s.a. 1011; ed. D. Whitelock, p. 91.

6. E.H.D. i, no. 127, pp. 545–7.

7. *Anglo-Saxon Chronicle*, s.a. 1006.

8. E.H.D. i, nos. 12 and 13: *Olafsdrapa* and *Eiriksdrapa*.

9. *Encomium Emmae*, ed. A. Campbell, London, 1949, p. 12; newly translated by Antonia Gransden, *Historical Writing in England c. 550 to 1307*, London, 1974, pp. 57–8.

10. E.H.D. i, pp. 855–9, particularly pp. 857–8.

11. *ibid.*, p. 414.

12. LIEBERMANN, *Die Gesetze*, i, pp. 274–5: E.H.D. i, pp. 414–16, especially cl. 13.

13. *Encomium Emmae*, ed. A. Campbell, p. 36, newly translated by Antonia Gransden, p. 59.

14. *Anglo-Saxon Chronicle* (C), s.a. 1030: ed. D. Whitelock, p. 101.

15. LIEBERMANN, *Die Gesetze*, i, pp. 276–7: E.H.D. i, pp. 416–18. P. Sawyer, *The Age of the Vikings* (2nd ed.), London, 1971, p. 34.

16. *Encomium Emmae*, ed. A. Campbell, pp. 34–5: *Danomarchiae, Angliae, Britanniae, Scothiae, Norduuegae vendicato dominio, imperator extitit. Britannia* clearly means Wales in this context.

17. *Anglo-Saxon Chronicle*, (C), s.a. 1042.

18. SIR FRANK STENTON, *Anglo-Saxon England* (3rd ed.) Oxford, 1971, pp. 574–5.

19. *Anglo-Saxon Chronicle*, (C), s.a. 1066: ed. D. Whitelock, pp. 144–5, and reference to the important note by Bruce Dickins 'The Late Addition to ASC 1066 C', *Proceedings of the Leeds Phil. and Lit. Soc.*, v. (1940), pp. 148 ff.

20. G. N. L. BROOKE, *London 800–1216: the Shaping of a City*, London, 1975, pp. 261–5, and pp. 287–8. Also Stenton, *Anglo-Saxon England*, p. 541.

Chapter 6

1. SIR JOHN LLOYD, *A History of Wales*, London, 1911, pp. 351–2.

2. *Annales Cambriae*, ed. J. Williams ab Ithel, London (Rolls Series), 1860, s.a. 999; Giraldus Cambrensis, ed. J. S. Brewer, J. F. Dimock, and G. F. Warner, London (Rolls Series), 1861–91; vol. vi (1868), ii, ch. 1, p. 104.

3. B. G. CHARLES, *Old Norse Relations with Wales*, Cardiff, 1934, p. 33: as a result of this defeat Maredudd ab Owain was forced to retreat to his southern kingdom of Deheubarth – *Annales Cambriae* s.a. 987.

4. *The History of Gruffydd ap Cynan*, ed. A. Jones, Manchester, 1910, pp. 102–3.

5. DONNCHA O'CORRAIN, *Ireland before the Normans*, Dublin, 1972, pp. 128–31.

6. T. D. KENDRICK, *A History of the Vikings*, London, 1930 (new impression, 1968), pp. 307–8.

7. ed. F. T. WAINWRIGHT, *The Northern Isles*, London, 1962, pp. 158–9.

8. ARNE JOHNSEN, 'The Payments from the Hebrides and Isle of Man to the crown of Norway, 1153–1263', and Barbara Crawford, 'The Pawning of Orkney and Shetland', *Scottish Historical Review*, xlviii, 1969, pp. 18–34 and 35–53, are indispensable to modern investigation.

Chapter 7

1. GUSTAVE REESE, *Music in the Middle Ages*, London, 1941, p. 387. I am grateful to Miss Drazek for drawing my attention to this reference.

2. *The Saga of Gunnlaug Serpent-Tongue*, ed. and trs. P. G. Foote and R. Quirk, London, 1957, p. 15.

3. D. WHITELOCK, *Sermo Lupi ad Anglos*, London (3rd ed.), 1963, pp. 37–45.

4. P. HUNTER BLAIR, *An Introduction to Anglo-Saxon England*, Cambridge, 1956, p. 192 and Plate XII.

5. *The Place-Names of Cumberland*, pt. 3 III, ed. Bruce Dickins, Cambridge, 1952, pp. xxvii–xxx. F. E. Harmer, *Anglo-Saxon Writs*, Manchester, 1952, pp. 419–24. F. M. Stenton, *Royal Commission on Historical Monuments (Westmorland)*, London, 1936, pp. xlviii–liii.

6. R. I. PAGE, *An Introduction to English Runes*, London, 1973, p. 198. This paragraph has relied heavily on Dr Page's work including his essay 'How long did the Scandinavian Language survive in England? The Epigraphical Evidence', *England before the Conquest*, ed. P. Clemoes and K. Hughes, Cambridge, 1971, pp. 165–81. Also E. V. Gordon, *Introduction to Old Norse* (2nd ed. rev. A. R. Taylor), O.U.P., 1957, pp. 185–6 for the Kirk Michael and Maeshowe inscriptions (alternative reading to Maeshowe in P. M. C. Kermode, *Catalogue of the Manks Crosses* (2nd ed.), Isle of Man, 1892, pp. 49–51; also

D. M. Wilson 'Manx Memorial Stones of the Viking period', *Saga-book of the Viking Society*, xviii, 1970–1, pp. 1–18.

7. OTTO JESPERSEN, *Growth and Structure of the English Language*, Oxford, 1935, remains a good general guide.

8. The essential modern studies on which the following paragraphs rely heavily are Gillian Fellows Jensen, *Scandinavian Personal Names in Lincolnshire and Yorkshire*, Copenhagen, 1968 and *Scandinavian Settlement Names in Yorkshire*, Copenhagen, 1972 (both with full bibliographies), and the work of K. Cameron, now conveniently gathered together in the relevant sections of *Place-name Evidence for the Anglo-Saxon Invasion and Scandinavian Settlements*, pp. 115–71, E.P.N.S., Nottingham, 1975.

9. GILLIAN FELLOWS JENSEN, 'Place-Name Research and Northern History: a Survey', *Northern History*, vii, Leeds, 1973, pp. 1–23, especially pp. 17–18. Dr Jensen draws attention to the papers of Bertil Hedevind (on Dentdale), Uppsala, 1967, A. Janzen (rejecting Yorkshire inversion compounds), *Names* (1957–63), and W. H. Pearsall (on ecological evidence in Cumberland), *Namn och Bygd*, 1961.

10. M. F. WAKELIN, *English Dialects. An Introduction*, London, 1972. J. Geipel, *The Viking Legacy. The Scandinavian Influence on the English and Gaelic Languages*, London, 1971, G. Kristensson, *A Survey of Middle English Dialects*, Lund, 1967, and E. Kolb 'Skandinavisches in den Nordenglischen Dialekten, *Anglia*, 83, 1965, pp. 127–53.

11. PETER SAWYER, 'The two Viking Ages of Britain. A Discussion', *Medieval Scandinavia* 2, 1969 (with contributions by among others K. Cameron, R. H. M. Dolley, and Lucien Musset) provides a lively introduction to the debate. The basic studies are Sir Frank Stenton, 'The Danes in England', *Proc. Brit. Acad.*, 1928, R. H. C. Davis, 'East Anglia and the Danelaw', *Trans. R. Hist. Soc.*, 1955, the work of Sawyer himself, notably the *Age of the Vikings* (2nd ed.), London, 1971, and the work of Gillian Fellows Jensen and K. Cameron referred to above.

12. *Chronicon Abbatiae Rameseiensis*, ed. W. D. Macray, Rolls Series, London, 1886, pp. 129–34 and 135–8. Antonia Gransden *Historical Writing in England*, London, 1974, p. 25. Also C. E. Wright, *The Cultivation of Saga in Anglo-Saxon England*, London, 1939, pp. 36–8 for comparable Ely material.

13. E.H.D. i, p. 399: Edgar IV, a code issued 962–3, soon after the plague of 962.

14. *ibid.*, p. 403: Ethelred III (978–1008), issued at Wantage. The 'English' code was issued at Woodstock.

15. *ibid.*, pp. 432–3 and 434–9.

16. *ibid.*, p. 403 (cl. 3.1) and p. 405 (cl. 13.2). *Anglo-Saxon Charters*, ed. A. J. Robertson, Cambridge, 1939, xxxix and especially xl (a list of

sureties for Peterborough estates). D. M. Stenton, *English Justice between the Norman Conquest and the Great Charter*, London, 1965, pp. 124–37 (illustrating the office of sacrabar) and pp. 55–6. Sir Frank Stenton, Anglo-Saxon England (3rd ed.), Oxford, 1971, pp. 512–13.

17. SIR FRANK STENTON, *op. cit.*, pp. 507–8, gives the best general account. E.H.D. i, pp. 408–9, Ethelred v, 32 (and note on Corpus manuscript); p. 421, Cnut II, 15–1a, 15.3.

18. References to the fundamental studies of Stenton himself on the Northern Danelaw and of D. C. Douglas on East Anglia are given in Sir Frank Stenton, *Anglo-Saxon England*, pp. 514–15.

19. H. R. LOYN, *Anglo-Saxon England and the Norman Conquest*, London, 1962, p. 55. R. Lennard, *Rural England*, 1086–1135, Oxford, 1959, is indispensable.

20. 'The Danes in England', *Proc. Brit. Acad.*, 1928.

21. R. H. C. DAVIS, 'East Anglia and the Danelaw', *Trans. R. Hist. Soc.*, 1955; G. C. Homans 'The Frisians in East Anglia', *Econ. H.R.*, 1957.

22. *Historians of the Church of York*, i, ed. J. Raine, Rolls Series, 1879; *Vita Oswaldi* (by a monk of Ramsey), p. 454.

23. The work of R. H. M. Dolley (ed.) *Anglo-Saxon Coins*, London, 1961, and much detailed analysis, notably in the *British Numismatic Journal* and the *Numismatic Chronicle* is central to modern investigation. See also Veronica Smart 'Moneyers of the Late Anglo-Saxon Coinage, 973–1016', *Commentationes de Nummis Saeculorum IX–XI in Suecia Repertis*, II, Stockholm, 1968, pp. 191–276.

24. C. N. L. BROOKE, *London 800–1216: the Shaping of a City*, London, 1975, pp. 267–8.

25. SIGURDUR THORARINSSON, *The Thousand Years Struggle Against Ice and Fire*, Reykjavik, 1956, p. 26.

26. ed. F. T. WAINWRIGHT, *The Northern Isles*, Edinburgh, 1962, pp. 120–6 (with references to the standard works by Jakobsen and Marwick), and pp. 144–5.

27. *ibid.*, pp. 124–6, where a fuller list of elements is given in reliable and convenient form.

28. KENNETH JACKSON, 'Common Gaelic: the evolution of the Goidelic Languages', *Proc. Brit. Acad.*, 1951, p. 77.

29. *ibid.*, pp. 78–80. Some of the fundamental brilliant work on the relationship between Scottish Gaelic and Manx appears in T. F. O'Rahilly, *Irish Dialects, Past and Present*, Dublin, 1932 (reproduced Dublin, 1972, with improved index), pp. 128–41.

30. ARNE JOHNSON and Barbara Crawford, *Scottish H.R.*, xlviii, 1969, pp. 18–34 and 35–53. See note 8 to chapter 6 above.

31. T. F. O'RAHILLY, *op. cit.*, especially p. 128 and pp. 137–8.

32. K. JACKSON, *Contributions to the Study of Manx Phonology*, London, 1955; M. Gelling, 'The place-names of the Isle of Man', *Journal of Manx Museum*, vii, 1970, pp. 130–9; and D. M. Wilson, *The Viking Age in the Isle of Man: the archaeological evidence*, Odense, 1974.

33. G. HAFSTRÖM, 'Atlantic and Baltic Earldoms', *Proceedings of the Sixth Viking Congress*, ed. P. G. Foote and D. Strömbäck, London, 1971, pp. 61–7.

34. *ibid.*, pp. 62–4; this paragraph is based on Hafström's analysis.

35. KENNETH JACKSON, 'The Celtic Languages during the Viking period', *Proc. International Congress of Celtic Studies*, Dublin, 1962, p. 9.

36. B. O'RIORDAIN, 'Excavations at High Street and Winetavern Street, Dublin', *Medieval Archaeology*, xv, 1971, pp. 73–85 and supplementary reports, *ibid.*, xvi, p. 168, xvii, pp. 151–2.

37. This paragraph draws heavily from Kathleen Hughes, *The Church in Early Irish Society*, London, 1966, pp. 253–74.

38. A summary of recent investigation appears in my Dorothea Coke Memorial Lecture, *The Vikings in Wales*, London, 1977.

39. ed. N. F. BLAKE, *The Saga of the Jomsvikings*, London, 1962. A discussion initiated by Rolf Arvidsson 'Source-Criticism and Literary History', *Medieval Scandinavia*, 5, 1972, has much pertinent material on the Jomsvikings.

40. MELVILLE RICHARDS, 'Norse Place-Names in Wales', *Proc. of the International Congress of Celtic Studies*, Dublin, 1962, pp. 55–9. B. G. Charles, *Old Norse Relations with Wales*, Cardiff, 1934, and *Non-Celtic Place-Names in Wales*, London, 1938, provide the fundamental modern guides.

Bibliography

The following bibliography of secondary works is by no means inclusive, but is calculated to give a general guide to the studies used in the construction of this book. The relevant sections of the *Annual Bulletin of the Historical Association,* and *British Archaeological Abstracts,* and the guides given in journals such as *Medieval Archaeology,* the *Saga-book of the Viking Society for Northern Research* and *Medieval Scandinavia,* provide the most convenient means of keeping in touch with this rapidly developing field of historical and archaeological study.

Abbreviations follow the standard pattern (Econ. H.R. for *Economic History Review,* E.H.R. for *English Historical Review,* Trans. R. Hist. Soc. for *Transactions of the Royal Historical Society,* etc.). E.H.D. i is used as a convenient abbreviation for ed. D. Whitelock, *English Historical Documents,* vol. i, London, 1955.

Bertil Almgren, *The Vikings,* London 1966.

ed. B. Almqvist and David Greene, Proceedings of the 7th Viking Congress, Dublin (1973), Dublin, 1976.

H. Arbman, *The Vikings,* trs. A. L. Binns, London, 1961.

G. W. S. Barrow, *The Kingdom of the Scots,* London, 1973.

Jakob Benediktsson, 'Landnamabok', *Saga-book of the Viking Society,* xvii, 1969.

Gerhard Bersu and D. M. Wilson, *Three Viking Graves in the Isle of Man,* London, 1966.

A. L. Binns, *The Viking Century in East Yorkshire,* York, 1963.

E. Björkman, *Scandinavian Loanwords in Middle English,* Hallé, 1900–2.

P. Hunter Blair, *An Introduction to Anglo-Saxon England,* Cambridge, 1956.

A. W. Brögger, *Ancient Emigrants: a history of the Norse Settlements in Scotland*, Oxford, 1929.

A. W. Brögger and Haaken Shetelig, *The Viking Ships*, trs. K. John, (reprint 1971), London, 1951.

Johannes Brøndsted, *The Vikings*, trs. K. Skov, London, 1960.

F. W. Brooks, *Domesday Book and the East Riding*, York, 1966.

F. J. Byrne, 'Ireland before the Norman invasion', *Irish Historical Studies*, 16, 1968.

Kenneth Cameron, *Place-Name Evidence for the Anglo-Saxon Invasion and Scandinavian Settlements* (8 Studies collected by G. K. Cameron with introduction by Margaret Gelling), E.P.N.S., 1975.

These include the three basic studies listed immediately below:

1. Kenneth Cameron 'Scandinavian Settlement in the Territory of the Five Boroughs: the Place-Name Evidence', Inaugural Lecture, University of Nottingham, 1965.
2. Kenneth Cameron 'Scandinavian Settlement in the Territory of the Five Boroughs: The Place-Name Evidence, Part II: Place-Names in Thorp', *Medieval Scandinavia*, iii, 1970.
3. Kenneth Cameron 'Scandinavian Settlement in the Territory of the Five Boroughs: The Place-Name Evidence, Part III, the Grimston-hybrids', *England before the Conquest*, ed. P. Clemoes and K. Hughes, Cambridge, 1971.

A. Campbell, *Skaldic Verses and Anglo-Saxon History*, London, 1971.

B. G. Charles, *Old Norse Relations with Wales*, Cardiff, 1934.

B. G. Charles, *Non-Celtic Place-Names in Wales*, London, 1938.

ed. P. Clemoes and K. Hughes, *England before the Conquest*, Cambridge, 1971.

Rosemary Cramp, *Anglian and Viking York*, York, 1968.

Barbara Crawford, 'The Earldom of Orkney and Lordship of Shetland: a Reinterpretation of their Pledging to Scotland in 1468–70', *Saga-book of the Viking Society*, xvii, London, 1967–8.

Barbara Crawford, 'The Pawning of Orkney and Shetland: a reconsideration of the events of 1460–9', *Scottish H.R.*, xlviii, 1969.

R. H. C. Davis, 'East Anglia and the Danelaw', *Trans. R. Hist. Soc.*, 1955.

R. H. M. Dolley, 'Some Reflections on Hildebrand Type A of Ethelred II', *Antikvariskt Arkiv* 9, Stockholm, 1958.

ed. R. H. M. Dolley, *Anglo-Saxon Coins*, London, 1961.

R. H. M. Dolley, *Anglo-Saxon Pennies*, London, 1964.

R. H. M. Dolley, *Viking Coins of the Danelaw and of Dublin*, London, 1965.

R. H. M. Dolley, *The Norman Conquest and the English Coinage*, London, 1966.

R. H. M. Dolley, *The Hiberno-Norse Coins in the British Museum*, London, 1966.

D. C. Douglas, *The Social Structure of Medieval East Anglia*, Oxford, 1927.

A. A. M. Duncan, *Scotland, the Making of the Kingdom*, Edinburgh, 1975.

Eilert Ekwall, *Scandinavians and Celts in the North-West of England*, Lund, 1918.

Eilert Ekwall, *Studies on English place- and personal names*, Lund, 1931.

English Place-Names Society. County surveys relating to the Danelaw include A. H. Smith's volumes on Yorkshire, K. Cameron's on Derbyshire, and F. M. Stenton's (*et al.*) on Nottinghamshire.

P. G. Foote and D. M. Wilson, *The Viking achievement: the society and culture of early medieval Scandinavia*, London, 1970.

ed. P. G. Foote and Dag Strömbäch, *Sixth Viking Congress, Uppsala, 1969*, Uppsala and London, 1971.

G. N. Garmonsway, *Canute and his Empire*, Dorothea Coke Memorial Lecture, 1963, London, 1964.

J. Geipel, *The Viking Legacy. The Scandinavian Influence on the English and Gaelic Languages*, London, 1971.

M. Gelling, 'The place-names of the Isle of Man', *The Journal of the Manx Museum*, vii, 1970.

E. V. Gordon, *An Introduction to Old Norse*, Oxford, 1927 (2nd rev. ed. by A. R. Taylor, 1957).

R. A. Hall, *The Viking Kingdom of York*, York, 1976.

Isabel Henderson, *The Picts*, London, 1967.

Françoise Henry, *Irish Art during the Viking Invasions (800–1020 A.D.)*, London, 1967.

Gerhard Hafström, 'Atlantic and Baltic Earldoms', *Proceedings of the Sixth Viking Congress*, ed. P. Foote and D. Strömbäch, London, 1971.

G. C. Homans, 'The Frisians in East Anglia', *Econ. H.R.*, 1957.

Kathleen Hughes, *The Church in Early Irish Society*, London, 1966.

K. Jackson, 'Common Gaelic: the Evolution of the Goidelic Languages', *Proc. Brit. Acad.*, 1951.

K. Jackson, 'The Celtic Languages during the Viking Period', *Proc. of International Congress of Celtic Studies*, Dublin, 1962.

J. Jakobsen, *Etymological Dictionary of the Norn Language in Shetland*, 2 vols., London and Copenhagen, 1928–32.

J. Jakobsen, *The Place-Names of Shetland*, London and Copenhagen, 1936.

Sven Jansson, *Swedish Vikings in England. The Evidence of the Rune Stones*, Dorothea Coke Memorial Lecture, London, 1966.

Gillian Fellows Jensen, *Scandinavian personal names in Lincolnshire and Yorkshire*, Copenhagen, 1968.

Bibliography

Gillian Fellows Jensen, *Scandinavian Settlement Names in Yorkshire*, Copenhagen, 1972.

Gillian Fellows Jensen, 'Place-name Research and Northern History: A Survey', *Northern History*, vii, Leeds, 1973.

Gillian Fellows Jensen, 'The Vikings in England: A review', *Anglo-Saxon England*, 4, C.U.P., 1975.

Arne Johnsen, 'The payments from the Hebrides and the Isle of Man to the crown of Norway', *Scottish H.R.*, xlviii, 1969.

Glanville R. J. Jones, 'Early Territorial Organisation in Northern England and its bearing on the Scandinavian Settlement', *The Fourth Viking Congress* (1961), ed. A. Small, London, 1965.

Gwyn Jones, *The Norse Atlantic Saga*, Oxford, 1964.

Gwyn Jones, *A History of the Vikings*, Oxford, 1968.

T. D. Kendrick, *A History of the Vikings*, London, 1930 (new impression 1968).

P. M. C. Kermode, *Manx Crosses*, London, 1907.

E. Kolb, 'Skandinavisches in den Nordenglischen Dialekten', *Anglia*, 83, 1965.

E. Kolb, 'The Scandinavian Loanwords in English and the Date of the West Norse Change MP > PP, NT > TT, NK > KK, *English Studies*, 50, 1969.

G. Kristensson, *A survey of Middle English Dialects*, Lund, 1967.

G. Kristensson, *Studies on Middle English Topographical Terms*, Lund, 1970.

Knud J. Krogh, *Viking Greenland*, Copenhagen, 1967.

H. H. Lamb, *Climate Present, Past, and Future*, vol. i, London, 1972. (Fundamentals and Climate Now.)

H. E. Landsberg (gen. ed.), *General Climatology*, vol. ii, ed. H. Flohn, Amsterdam, 1969. (Ch. 5, 'Climatic Fluctuations' by H. H. Lamb.)

R. Lennard, *Rural England, 1086–1135*, Oxford, 1959.

Sir John Lloyd, *History of Wales*, two vols., London, 1911.

H. R. Loyn, *Anglo-Saxon England and the Norman Conquest*, London, 1962.

H. R. Loyn, 'Anglo-Saxon Stamford', *The Making of Stamford*, ed. A. Rogers, Leicester, 1965.

H. R. Loyn and J. Percival, *The Reign of Charlemagne*, London, 1975.

H. R. Loyn, *The Vikings in Wales*, Dorothea Coke Memorial Lecture, London, 1977.

A. T. Lucas, 'Irish-Norse Relations: Time for a Reappraisal?', *J. of the Cork Hist. and Arch. Soc.*, 1966.

A. T. Lucas, 'The Plundering and Burning of Churches in Ireland, 7th to 10th Century', *North Munster Studies*, ed. E. Rynne, Limerick, 1967.

C. S. S. Lyon, 'Historical Problems of Anglo-Saxon Coinage: the Viking Age', B.N.J., 1970.

Magnus Magnusson, *Viking Expansion Westwards*, London, 1973.

Brita Malmer, *King Canute's Coinage in the Northern Countries*, Dorothea Coke Memorial Lecture, London, 1974.

H. Marwick, *The Orkney Norn*, Oxford, 1929.

H. Marwick, *Orkney Farm-Names*, Kirkwall, 1952.

D. M. Metcalf, 'The Prosperity of North-Western Europe in the Eighth and Ninth Centuries', *Econ. H.R.*, 1967.

ed. D. Moore, *The Irish Sea Province in Archaeology and History*, Cardiff, 1970.

L. Musset, *Les Invasions: le Second Assaut contre l'Europe Chrétienne (VIIIe–XIe siècles)*, Paris, 1965.

L. Musset, 'La pénétration chrétienne dans l'Europe du nord et son influence sur la civilisation scandinave', *La conversione al cristianesimo nell' Europa dell' alto medioevo*, Spoleto, 1967.

W. F. H. Nicolaisen, 'Norse settlement in the Northern and Western Isles', *Scottish H.R.*, xlviii, 1969.

W. F. H. Nicolaisen, *Scottish Place-names*, London, 1976.

D. O'Corrain, *Ireland before the Normans*, Dublin, 1972.

Olaf Olsen and Ole Crumlin-Pedersen, 'The Skuldelev Ships', *Acta Archaeologia*, 1967.

Olaf Olsen, *Horgr, Hof and Church*, Copenhagen, 1966.

Olaf Olsen, 'The Geometrical Viking Fortresses', *Château Gaillard IV*, ed. A. L. J. van de Walle, Ghent, 1968.

Eric Oxenstierna, *The World of the Norsemen*, London, 1957.

Eric Oxenstierna, *The Norsemen*, (trs. C. Hutter), London, 1966.

R. I. Page, 'How long did the Scandinavian language survive in England? The epigraphical evidence', *England before the Conquest*, ed. P. Clemoes and K. Hughes, Cambridge, 1971.

R. I. Page, *An Introduction to English Runes*, London, 1973.

W. H. Pearsall, 'Place-Names as Clues in Pursuit of Ecological History', *Namn och Bygd*, 1961.

Proceedings of the International Congress of Celtic Studies (1959), Dublin, 1962.

Gustave Reese, *A History of Medieval Music*, London, 1941.

Melville Richards, 'Norse Place-Names in Wales', *Proc. of International Congress of Celtic Studies*, Dublin, 1962.

Else Roesdahl, 'The Viking Fortress of Fyrkat in the light of the objects found', *Château Gaillard VI*, ed. M. de Bouard, Caen, 1973.

P. H. Sawyer, 'The Density of the Danish Settlement in England', Univ. of Birmingham Historical Journal, vi, 1958.

P. H. Sawyer, *The Age of the Vikings,* London, 1962, (second rev. ed. 1971).

P. H. Sawyer, 'The Wealth of England in the Eleventh Century', *Trans. R. Hist. Soc.,* 1965.

D. J. Schove, 'Climatic Fluctuations in Europe in the Late Historical Period, 800–1700', M.Sc. Thesis, Geography, London, 1953.

Scottish H.R., xlviii, 1969. The whole number (No. 145, April 1969) is devoted to a series of important studies commemorative of the Union of Orkney and Shetland with Scotland.

Haakon Shetelig, *An Introduction to the Viking History of Western Europe. Viking Antiquities in Great Britain and Ireland,* Oslo, 1940.

Jacqueline Simpson, *Everyday Life in the Viking Age,* London, 1967.

ed. Alan Small, *The Fourth Viking Congress,* Aberdeen and London, 1965.

Alan Small, 'The Distribution of Settlement in Shetland and Faroe in Viking Times', *Saga-book of the Viking Society,* xvii, 1967–8.

A. H. Smith, *English Place-Name Elements,* (E.P.N.S.), Cambridge, 1956.

A. P. Smyth, *Scandinavian York and Dublin,* Dublin, 1975.

D. M. Stenton, *English Justice between the Norman Conquest and the Great Charter,* London, 1965.

ed. D. M. Stenton, *Preparatory to Anglo-Saxon England,* Oxford, 1970.

F. M. Stenton, *Types of Manorial Structure in the Northern Danelaw,* Oxford, 1910.

F. M. Stenton, 'The Danes in England, ' *Proc. of the Brit. Acad.,* 1928.

F. M. Stenton, 'The Historical Bearing of Plane-Name Studies: the Danish Settlement of Eastern England', *Trans. R. Hist. Soc.,* xxiv, 1942.

F. M. Stenton, 'The Scandinavian Colonies in England and Normandy', *Trans. R. Hist. Soc.,* xxvii, 1945.

F. M. Stenton, *Anglo-Saxon England,* (3rd ed. by D. M. Stenton), Oxford, 1971.

Dag Strömbäch, *The Conversion of Iceland,* (trs. P. Foote), Viking Society for Northern Research, London, 1975.

C. H. V. Sutherland, *English Coinage,* London, 1973.

Sigurdur Thorarinsson, *The Thousand Years Struggle against Ice and Fire,* (Museum of Natural History, Misc. Papers 14), Reykjavik, 1956.

E. O. G. Turville-Petre, *The Heroic Age of Scandinavia,* London, 1951.

E. O. G. Turville-Petre, *Myth and Religion of the North,* London, 1964.

G. Utterström, 'Climatic Fluctuations and Population Problems in early Modern History', *Scand. Econ. H.R.,* iii, 1955.

F. T. Wainwright, *Archaeology and Place-names in the period A.D. 400–1100,* London, 1962.

ed. F. T. Wainwright, *The Northern Isles,* London, 1962.

M. F. Wakelin, *English Dialects. An Introduction*, London, 1972.

J. M. Wallace-Hadrill, *Early Germanic Kingship in England and on the Continent*, Oxford, 1971.

Dorothy Whitelock, 'The Conversion of the Eastern Danelaw', *Saga-book of the Viking Society for Northern Research*, xii, London, 1941.

ed. Dorothy Whitelock, *English Historical Documents*, vol. i, London, 1955, (E.H.D. i).

Dorothy Whitelock, 'The Dealings of the Kings of England with Northumbria in the Tenth and Eleventh Centuries', *The Anglo-Saxons*, ed. P. Clemoes, London, 1959.

ed. Dorothy Whitelock, *The Anglo-Saxon Chronicle*, London, 1961.

ed. Dorothy Whitelock, *Sermo Lupi ad Anglos*, London (3rd ed.), 1963.

Dorothy Whitelock (ed. and trs.), *The Will of Aethelgifu*, Oxford (Roxburgh Club), 1968.

D. M. Wilson *Anglo-Saxon Ornamental Metalwork, 700–1100, in the British Museum*, London, 1964.

D. M. Wilson and O. Klindt-Jensen, *Viking Art*, London, 1966.

D. M. Wilson, 'The Vikings' Relationship with Christianity in Northern England', *Journal of the Archaeological Association*, xxx, 1967.

D. M. Wilson, 'Archaeological evidence for the Viking settlements and raids in England', *Frühmittelalterliche Studien* 2, 1968.

D. M. Wilson, *The Vikings and their Origins*, London, 1970.

D. M. Wilson, *The Viking Age in the Isle of Man: the archaeological evidence*, Odense, 1974.

D. M. Wilson, 'Scandinavian Settlement in the North and West of the British Isles: An Archaeological Point-of-view', *Trans. R. Hist. Soc.*, 1976.

ed. D. M. Wilson, *The Archaeology of Anglo-Saxon England*, London, 1976.

C. E. Wright, *The Cultivation of Saga in Anglo-Saxon England*, London, 1939.

H. C. Wyld, *A Short History of English*, 3rd ed., Oxford, 1925.

Index